a different life

Quinn Bradlee
with Jeff Himmelman

a different life
growing up
learning disabled
and other
adventures

a memoir

PUBLICAFFAIRS
New York

Published in the United States by PublicAffairs™, a member of the
Perseus Books Group.

Book Design by Pauline Brown
Text set in 11.5 point New Baskerville

Library of Congress Cataloging-in-Publication Data
Bradlee, Quinn.
A different life / Quinn Bradlee with Jeff Himmelman.
p.   cm.
ISBN 978-1-58648-189-6 (hardcover)
1. Bradlee, Quinn. 2. Velocardiofacial syndrome—Patients—Biography.
I. Himmelman, Jeff. II. Title.
RB155.5.B73 2009
616'.042092—dc22
[B]
2008039570

First Edition

10 9 8 7 6 5 4 3 2 1

To my friend and listener Justin Lee Peterson.

To the greatest parents in the world and my greatest supporters—my mom, who is my archangel, and my father, who is my sword and shield.

This book is also dedicated to my maternal grandparents—Lt. Gen. William Wilson "Buffalo Bill" Quinn (Dandy), who taught me to always keep fighting through life, and Sara Bette Williams Quinn (Nana), who spoiled me rotten, taught me how to swear, and was the greatest cook in the world.

To my paternal grandparents, whom I never met— Frederick Josiah Bradlee, Jr. (Grandpa), who went from having everything to nothing but kept on living for his children, and Josephine deGersdorff (Granny), who protected the innocent children of WWII and gave them shelter.

And to all those who have learning disabilities.

Contents

Our family in the early days.

a different life

How It Feels, Take One

————

  I feel like I'm always in a battle. It's Omaha Beach, and they're shooting bullets at you from above. The guys on the cliff who are shooting at you are the people who never had a problem. I'm dodging bullets all the time. Sometimes I feel like a soldier from the Civil War. You're holding your old musket, but you realize it's modern times. And the enemy is expectation. I'm always fighting expectation. Sometimes it feels like battle after battle, day after day.

How It Feels,
Take Two

Surfing is a lot harder than it looks. But there was something that was telling me to keep on doing it. A religious type of feeling, a spiritual type of feeling—something. Nobody can really help you do it, either. You have to do it yourself. Somebody can open the door for you, but you have to walk through it. Sometimes I'm scared of working hard to become good at something. What if I fail? But with surfing I said, "I'm going to learn how to do this if it kills me."

And when you ride that wave, you conquer that wave when you've caught it, but you become part of it, too. It's just like conquering a part of your life. It's knowing that you can do things that you'd never thought you would be able to do, like an invitation to become something greater than who you are. It's a sense of accomplishment that doesn't happen to me a lot. It's the greatest feeling that you can get.

The Story

I was born with a hole in my heart. They had to open my chest when I was three months old to fix it. Most of what I remember of being young are hospitals. I was always in there for something: seizures, migraines, fevers, tests, re-tests, whatever. I spent more time being sick than I did in school some years. At least it felt that way.

And when I was in school, I had some trouble there, too. Nobody ever knew what was "wrong" with me, and I got passed around. A lot of people told me and my parents that I'd never do a lot of the things that I've done. One of my favorite things in life is proving those people wrong.

When I was fourteen, I was diagnosed with velo-cardio-facial syndrome (VCFS). VCFS is a genetic syndrome, but most of the time it occurs in children of "normal" parents. It affects about 1 in 2,000 people worldwide, making it the second-most-common syndrome after Down syndrome. The main symptoms of VCFS are trouble with your heart, some trouble with your speech, and learning disabilities. There are also more than 180 physical symptoms, everything from scoliosis to tapering fingers, and each person who has the syndrome has a different mix. Some people never even know they have VCFS, and some people have it so bad that they don't live through it. Mine is a pretty mild case. I guess that's why it took them so long to figure it out.

I'm writing this book because most people don't know anything about VCFS or what it's like to grow up with learning disabilities. When people ask if I'm learning disabled, I tell them that I'm dyslexic. This isn't technically true, but it's easier than explaining the whole syndrome. I do have trouble reading and processing what I read and hear, but that's not all. There are a lot of different symptoms of VCFS, so it's more complicated.

In the end there's nothing incredibly special about me. I'm just a kid who was born into a distinguished family, and so maybe I have a better chance than somebody else does to explain. Maybe I have more responsibility, too.

Last year I helped make a documentary called *Living with VCFS*. Now I have launched a Web site where kids and young adults with all different kinds of learning disabilities can go to talk to each other and form a community. (Or maybe just pick up chicks.) I wish I'd had something like that when I was younger. I'm hoping this book can help with that, too.

I couldn't have put this whole book together by myself, even though I know everything that I want to say. Over the past seven years, I had help from Kyle Gibson and Jeff Himmelman (who have interviewed me a lot), and from my parents, doctors, and some of my teachers. That's where most of this material comes from. I wrote some of it myself, but I didn't sit at the computer and arrange everything in this form. That's why I needed Jeff. Well, that and the free guitar lessons.

There are parts of my past that I don't remember, and parts of my medical history, too. I think when you have a tough time, you don't really *want* to remember. That's part of it as well. In those cases my mom and dad fill in the gaps, or my doctors. It's the only way I could really give you a complete picture.

I'm not a huge reader. But one of my favorite books of all time is *The Adventures of Huckleberry Finn*. I love the language. Twain writes like his characters would talk. That made it easier for me to understand. This book is how I talk. If Mark Twain did it, why can't I? I hope it turns out okay.

What an amazing difference between the Moderns and Ancients respecting the knowledge of navigation and geography! Here am I, a man from a new nation and a new world crossing the Atlantic Ocean, and entering the vestibule of the grand temple of the Mediterranean, where God has shown all his wonders, and produced changes among the inhabitants of the earth, that demand the profoundest researches and constant contemplation of man.

Here God has spoken to man, here he has shown his creatures his power, by new laws given to matter! Here he has instructed man in his duty and expectations, and here you see his predictions of the fate of Nations verified. When I think of these things in this place I tremble.

CAPT. GEORGE CROWNINSHIELD JR.,
my great-great-great-great uncle,
on board *Cleopatra's Barge*
May 7, 1817

My Ancestry

Anybody who knows me knows that I'm a little obsessed with my ancestry. I spend hours doing research on the Web and trying to figure out everybody I'm related to. I use ancestry.com a lot. I probably keep those guys in business.

Someday I want to write a whole book about it, but I know it's kind of hard to be interested in somebody else's family when you have nothing to do with it. One thing of interest that I discovered is that my grandparents on my dad's side were fourth cousins. Maybe that's why I came out a little funny.

But since this *is* my book, I do want to tell you a little bit about my heritage. I'm proud of my family and of being a part of it. Sometimes I feel a little out of place, that the only thing that sets me apart from anybody else is my disability. Tracing my family roots back, seeing that I'm part of a long line of strong men and women, usually makes me feel better.

My dad is Benjamin Crowninshield Bradlee, descended from a long line of Crowninshields through
both his mom and his dad. He was the editor of the
Washington Post for twenty-six years. (Jason Robards
played him in *All the President's Men*.) To me he's
mostly just my dad. I didn't realize how important
his job was for a long time, because he resigned as
the editor when I was nine and I never really saw
him in action. He is one of the most modest people
in the world.

One of the first times I realized that my dad was
kind of a big deal in Washington was at Kay Graham's funeral. She was the owner of the *Post* for a
long time, and like an aunt to me. She was a different kind of strong. There were a lot of famous
people at her funeral, and when my dad spoke, he
cheered up the whole church. I'm always proud that
he's my dad. He's great at cracking jokes and making other people feel good about themselves. But
on a day like Kay's funeral, I realize how much he
means to other people, too.

There were a lot of illustrious Crowninshields on
my dad's side. I won't bore you with all of them,
but Johann Kasper Richter von Kronenschieldt (try
saying that fast ten times) was the first to come to
America, so in a way he's one of my most significant
forebears. My dad's great uncle, Frank Crowninshield, founded *Vanity Fair* and nurtured a lot of lit-
erary talents, F. Scott Fitzgerald and e. e. cummings
among them.

My paternal grandmother, Josephine
deGersdorff, in a kilt.

My dad's mom was Josephine deGersdorff. The
most interesting thing about her is that during
World War II, she helped French children who were
sent to America to escape the war and the Nazis.
Because of her heroism, she was awarded the Legion
of Honor, which is the highest honor any civilian can
receive from the French government. (My mom's
dad received the same medal, and last year it was
awarded to my dad. Maybe someday I'll get it—or at
least here's hoping.) My paternal grandmother was

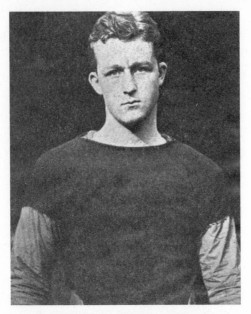

My grandfather, Frederick Josiah Bradlee, Jr.,
in his younger years as a football player.

also a great singer, and she could curse in German.
I'm sad that I never got to meet her.

I'm also sorry that I never met my dad's dad,
Frederick Josiah Bradlee Jr. Like most Bradlees
since about 1730, he went to Harvard. You can trace
Bradlees back to the 1630s, when John Bradley came
over from England. The story goes that the family
name became Bradlee when a man named Samuel
Bradley was running for office near Boston and
people kept confusing his name with another
Bradley. During the Revolutionary War, the British

had a royal warrant to arrest, and I believe shoot, any Bradlee.

My grandfather graduated from Harvard in 1915. He was an all-American on the football team, and his main position was fullback. Later in his life, he could apparently drink like a fish without ever getting hung over. (How he did this is a mystery to me. I wish I had inherited that ability.) He worked his family out of the Depression when it hit, with a series of odd jobs. And he was really cool about the fact that my dad's brother Freddy was gay. In those days I think that was probably pretty rare.

I was lucky to become really close with both of my mother's parents. My mom is Sally Sterling Quinn, Scotch-Irish, raised in Savannah, Georgia, and nobody to be messed with. Good luck if you want to try. My dad is basically retired, though he still goes into the office every day, but my mom is still a working journalist. I watch her ask people questions sometimes and she knows what she's doing. She also throws great parties. She's a powerful lady. If I had to sum her up all at once, I would say that she has been the archangel of my life, always pushing me.

My mom's mom was a Williams, and apparently we are related to William Williams of Connecticut, who was one of the fifty-six men who signed the Declaration of Independence. The biggest tragedy of the Williams side is that my great-grandfather,

My beloved Nana, hamming it up.

who was a respected surgeon in Savannah, was a friend of John Stith Pemberton, who invented Coca-Cola. John asked my great-granddad to try a sip of his new invention to see if he might want to invest. When he tried it, my great-granddad said he wouldn't give Pemberton one cent because it was the most awful taste he had ever put in his mouth. We could have been billionaires.

My grandma, Sara Bette Williams, was a southern belle from Savannah, Georgia. I called her Nana. In her obituary it was said that she had the sexiest legs in all of Savannah. She was also the best cook in the whole wide world from my experience, and the best grandmother. She basically cooked everything in butter or in bacon grease. Fattening, but man, was it good. I used to spend a night or two a week at my grandparents' apartment in D.C. when I was a kid, and Nana would call me "Dollbaby" and cook me whatever I wanted. Hard to beat.

On the Quinn side, we're descended from a young man named John Quinn, who came over from Belfast, Ireland, because he hated his step-mother. He decided to head for Jamestown to explore the new world, and was a stowaway on one of his father's ships, the *Falcon*. The ship wrecked on what is now known as Kent Island. Only two survivors, the sixteen-year-old Quinn and the ship's mate, were safely swept ashore by a wave to an oyster-shell beach. I guess the moral of the story is that John Quinn had balls, and he was a survivor. I'm happy to be able to claim him as an ancestor.

My mom's dad, "Dandy" to me but General William Wilson Quinn to everybody else, served in the army for a total of thirty-two years. He was one of the main people who oversaw the change of the OSS into the CIA, and in World War II his regiment captured the infamous Hermann Göring. On April 29 (which also happens to be my birthday), he liberated the German concentration camp of Dachau in 1945. He also helped to plan the invasion of southern France. In the Korean War, he was known as "Buffalo Bill." His troops were the

General William Wilson Quinn (Dandy), in
uniform.

Buffaloes, whose motto was "Truth and Courage."
Barry Goldwater was one of Dandy's best friends. He
was pretty badass.

One of my favorite stories about Dandy is that
when he was in high school, his principal told him
he didn't have what it took to make it to West Point.
Dandy worked his butt off and eventually got in,
and during his second year of college, he went back
in his uniform and paid that principal a little visit.
Some eating of words, I imagine. It was an example
in my family of somebody being told they couldn't

do something and doing it anyway, which is something that I try to do every day.

Dandy could also knock back some booze when he felt like it. One time when I was nine I was thirsty as hell and I reached for what I thought was a cold Coke on the table. Well, it wasn't a cold Coke. Or if it was, it sure had a lot of whiskey in it. I guess you could say that was my first drink. I thought I was going to throw up. I never made that mistake again.

Me on Dandy's lap.

I could go on about my family forever, but you get the point. A lot of them made significant contributions to society. I would like someday to contribute to their illustrious lineage. (I tried to sneak myself onto a list of "notable Crowninshields" once, just for shits and giggles, but they took me off pretty quick.) I know I won't be editor of the *Washington Post* or a famous journalist, but my family's legacy gives me something to strive for. I don't think it makes me better than anybody else. It just makes me want to *be* better.

I am the eighth generation Josiah Bradlee. I feel that that's a responsibility. I also feel pressure sometimes to live up to who my parents are. But there's a lot of good that comes with that, too. In the end I'm really grateful for where I come from.

Staying in touch with my Scottish roots.

Mr. Mellow

When I was first born, everyone thought I was totally and completely normal. According to my mom, the nurses called me "Mr. Mellow," because while all the other babies would scream and cry, I would just kind of look around. She also says that when she first had me in her arms, she told me that she loved me and that I could be anything I wanted to be in the world.

But pretty soon after I was born, my doctor detected a heart murmur, and when I was about three months old, I had to have open-heart surgery. (Heart defects are a pretty universal symptom of VCFS, but we didn't even know I had VCFS yet.) I had what's called a ventricular septal defect, where blood leaks from one side of your heart to the other. The doctors put a Dacron patch over the leak. It's a piece of durable plastic that stays there forever, and your heart grows around it.

I think this was a pretty crappy time for my parents. They thought I might die, and I could have

Baby me, safe in mom's arms.

died. My dad and the *Post* were getting sued by some guy, and I think the day I had surgery was the day that he had to go into court and he lost. (He eventually won, so it turned out okay, but that day he lost.) It was not a great time for anybody.

My mom says the night before my heart operation was one of the worst nights of her life. She wasn't allowed to nurse me. She could barely even hold me. When they took me into the operating room the next day, she basically fainted. Apparently my dad turned to her and said, "Just think of it this way. He'll never have to go to war."

Asleep on Dad's chest at the pharmacy.

My dad says that his favorite image of me is from just after the operation. My mom was on one side of me, and he was on the other, and I was holding their fingers. I was out cold, but my dad says that I held on, that I just held on and kept going. I don't know if I came through that surgery with flying colors or not, but I came through. I won't give up when it has something to do with my health. I still have a scar from that operation that goes more than halfway down my chest.

After the heart surgery, I was always sick with something. I think my parents thought that once they did the surgery I'd be fine, but it didn't work out that way. You should see my medical files. They're about six inches thick.

One thing that helped me make sense of my illnesses as a kid was that both my mom and my dad had almost died when they were young. It's like it runs in the family. My dad had polio, and he watched his friend die next to him in the ambulance on the way from school to the hospital. When her dad was fighting in Korea, my mom had to live for almost a whole year in a hospital in Japan. She was so scared for her dad at the front lines that she couldn't eat, and they had to keep her on an IV for months. At one point her appendix ruptured and she almost died. Her friend in the bed next to her actually passed away. So we've all faced it. And we're all fighters.

The first bad thing to come for me, after the heart surgery, were the seizures. A lot of them, starting when I was almost two. This is from a doctor's letter from just one of my many visits to Children's Hospital:

> This is a 26 month old male child with a four month history of seizures who the evening of admission had a fever which rose rapidly from normal to 104 degrees, at which point he was noted to have a grand mal seizure. He had been in his normal state of health until that afternoon, when he was noted to have a fever. The family gave him baths, Tylenol

times two but the fever continued to climb. Private MD was called who advised to continue the same therapy, after which the temperature continued to climb to 104. Child had a seizure and was brought to the emergency room here from where he was admitted. Since his arrival to the hospital he had one seizure in the emergency room and was seen by the senior resident who admitted him. There is a history of seizures since February of 1984, initially occurring at a rate of several per week.

I can only imagine how freaked out my parents must have been. Especially my mom, because she freaks out about everything. Also, they realized when I was around that age that my immune system was screwed up. Whenever an infection went around, I would get the worst version of it and end up with bronchitis or pneumonia.

By the time I was two, my parents could tell that I had some issues other than my health. They put me into a "regular" nursery school, but within a week the teachers told my mom that I couldn't hack it. They gave me my own tutor and everything, but it still didn't work. I started with speech therapy. The doctors did some testing on me for various known genetic conditions, but I didn't have anything anybody recognized.

I only really remember one hospital visit from this period. I was running around naked at our house in Washington and a bee stung me right where it hurts. There was some bad swelling involved. Not a very pleasant way to discover you are allergic to bee stings.

It was always something. I had surgery for a hernia. At one point I had a prolapsed lung, which means part of my lung was basically collapsed, and they thought it might be cystic fibrosis. I had to have what's called a sweat test, where they put these weird gloves on your hands and then test them afterwards. My mom says that the whole staff at Children's Hospital told her to pray that I didn't have it, because it would mean I would have died in my twenties. Luckily, the tests were negative.

I rarely felt totally healthy, and I was at the doctor's office constantly as a kid. My mom says she felt like she lived there. This description is from a doctor's visit when I was eight, and it's typical of many of my visits to the doctor during these years:

> Teacher describes Quinn as "out of it," cannot concentrate (spacey). Allergies, stomach ache, rash under arm and neck, temperature 100 last night.

It was constantly like that. And those were just the minor ones.

When I was about four, my parents put me into the Lab School, a new school for learning-disabled kids in Washington, D.C. I was the youngest kid there. I think I might have been the youngest kid ever to go there. But they were very welcoming to me.

Up until that time, there really weren't very many places for learning-disabled kids to go. The Lab School was the first place in Washington that was set up for somebody like me. I don't know what I would have done without it. Sally Smith, a great lady who recently passed away, founded the school, and the teaching focused on what kids *could* do, not what they couldn't. Lots of learning by doing, lots of art.

The truth is that I don't remember a lot of my particular experience at the Lab School, but I do remember my second- or third-grade teacher, Ms. Spruance. She was the best teacher in the world, and I was her pet. During class she would give me back rubs. My dad says I spent the entire year sitting in the prettiest teacher's lap, and that was about right. I would sit on her lap while all the other kids were doing work, and she'd just give me back rubs. She was really, really good to me. So was Neela Seldin, who was the head of the lower school and was always pretty forgiving when I got into trouble.

I also remember Sally Smith. When I was in grade school, I could always tell when she was coming around the corner. For one thing, she had a really big presence, but for another she wore the same perfume as my grandmother did. So I could always smell her when she was on her way, and it was like, "Okay, time to stop screwing around." Just another way Nana looked out for me, I guess.

*   *   *

When I was little, it was pretty clear to everybody that I had some problems speaking. I didn't really realize it, because my mom could understand me and I talked mostly to her. But I do remember one time we went to the drugstore, and I asked the guy for something, and he couldn't understand me. I asked him three more times, but he still didn't get it. I turned to my mom and asked, "What's *his* problem?" She loves to tell that story.

When it became clear that I was having real problems with my speech, I started daily speech therapy. I was only two or three at the time. When I was eight and nine, I had to have operations on my throat, on what is called the pharyngeal flap, to help me produce sound. The two procedures helped, but I think people still had trouble understanding me.

It was around this time that the Lab School sent me out to a psychiatrist or psychologist to have a look at me. I have no memory of the experience, but my parents sure do. After about six months, the woman called my parents in and basically told them that I was retarded. She'd done some tests, and she had determined that I was never going to be able to function as an adult in any meaningful way. Never graduate from high school, never even go to high school, never work or have a job or be married or have kids or any of the things you dream about. She told my parents they needed to put me in an institution in Maryland, where she had already reserved a spot for me.

I can't really imagine what my mom and dad felt like.

They wouldn't believe it, and they didn't tell me about it until much later. Luckily the Lab School didn't agree with this woman's assessment. They told my mom that the psychologist was wrong. I stayed there.

Just as I'd been dismissed as a lost cause by this therapist, my mom got a letter from Children's Hospital reporting that when I had had my open-heart surgery, I had gotten a blood transfusion. A bunch of the kids who had gotten blood transfusions at the time had since tested positive for HIV. My mom just about lost it again. The wait for the results of my HIV test was a week. My mom called the hospital so many times that they finally told her early.

When I was twelve, we went through the same thing again. Some kids who'd tested negative the first time had turned up positive. I didn't sweat it all that much, but it wasn't pleasant. Sure helps put your problems into perspective.

I feel a little bad that I don't remember much of this, because I wish I could describe it to you better, like how I felt at a given time—with the surgeries, or the HIV tests. But truthfully, I don't even really remember being a little kid. I only remember it when I see pictures of birthday parties and holidays. So we just have to make do with what I've got, which is mostly hospitals and tests kind of on a loop. In my next life I'm going to have a photographic memory.

As you might guess, my mom remembers everything about my childhood, to this day. I thought this might be a good place to have you hear what she has to say about when I was little, because it's a different perspective. It shows you what the parents go through, too, and that the problems I had as a kid didn't only affect me:

I remember the first seizure he had, in the front hall of our house. I didn't know what it was. I remember picking him up and the nanny got the car out of the garage, and I was standing on the front steps holding him, this completely lifeless, limp body. He had gone completely blue. His face had turned blue, his lips turned blue. And she pulled the car out front and I ran with his limp body and got in the backseat and just held him, held him all the way to the hospital.

And as he says here, he really was sick all the time, because he had and still does have a suppressed immune system. He couldn't have dental work or any invasive procedure at all without antibiotics. And it also meant that if anything was going around, he'd get it first and have it longer and have it worse than anybody else. He either had the flu or pneumonia all the time.

In some ways, we were lucky that Quinn was diagnosed with learning disabilities so early in life, when he was only a little more than three. He got to the special schools early. A lot of kids only get there after they've been completely humiliated and degraded and teased and bullied beyond endurance, or made to feel stupid and lazy and hopeless and

*everything else. He never had that experience. I think that
accounts for a lot of his confidence.*

*And he was so brave as a kid, through all of his sur-
geries. He never cried when he had surgery, never showed
any pain. Never cried. He would have to have blood tests
all the time. I had a terrible experience in a hospital in Japan when I was young—I was there for almost a year—and
so I basically faint when I get around needles.*

*So Quinn would walk in by himself. They had this
great phlebotomist who took his blood, this wonderful black
guy named Eddie. Quinn would sit in the chair and stick
his arm out, and Eddie would say, "Hey, that's my man."
And Quinn would have his blood taken. This went on
for years.*

*When he was eight, he went to this therapist for six or
eight months. Maybe six months. One day she called Ben
and me and she said, Well, I'm sorry, but I have to tell you
I've given Quinn a test. And the test showed that he is never
going to be able to function as a normal adult in any
way. You should know that he is going to be institutionalized, and he will never graduate from high school, he will
never go to high school, he will certainly never go to college
and he'll never be able to work or have a job or be married
or have children or function in any kind of way. And,
she says, I've taken the liberty of reserving a place for him
in this institution out in Maryland, and I've talked to the
Lab School, and they're all in agreement on this.*

*Total shock for us. Total shock. I mean, we couldn't
walk out of there. It was the first time I'd ever seen Ben just
lose it. And now, we don't know a single parent of an LD*

[learning disabled] kid who hasn't at some point had some idiot tell them something like this. This is a constant, constant nightmare of LD parents, who have their children misdiagnosed by idiots. This woman was an idiot.

We drove right over to the Lab School, once we stopped crying, and we stormed in there and said, "What is this? Why do we have to hear it from this person that you've agreed that he should be institutionalized?" And they said, "We don't know what you're talking about. We've never had a conversation with this woman." I wanted to report her, but I didn't. It took us quite a while to get over it. I'm sure you can imagine.

The advice I would give to other families is therapy. I mean it. Immediately. It's helped me a lot in seeing that it wasn't my fault, that I didn't do anything wrong. I also think it's important because husbands and wives deal with it differently. You can find statistics at Children's Hospital of parents who have a child who died, and the number who separate and divorce is unbelievable. It's not much less for people who have chronically ill children. The reason is that parents grieve differently. The mothers are all much more into it, much more open about their grief and their sadness and their depression. They want to talk about it and deal with it in the open. The men don't want to talk about it. They're often in denial. And that's true.

Porto
Bello

When I was sick all the time as a kid, Porto Bello was the one truly bright spot in my life. When I was about eight, my parents bought an old tobacco farm across the river from St. Mary's City, Maryland, about an hour and a half from our house in D.C. The house was built in 1740, and it is by far my favorite place in the world.

You drive in along a driveway that's about a mile long, through meadows and fields, and you can see the river. The first building you see is this big red barn with wide-open doors, out in the middle of one of the fields. It has always reminded me of myself because it's off on its own, away from all the other barns near the main house. It was like me being on my own, and all the cool kids are together somewhere else. I've always identified with it. My mom says it's the most beautiful barn of all.

The main house at Porto Bello is a historic manor house that my parents rebuilt and restored, and it sits on a peninsula surrounded by water. On

The barn at Porto Bello.

a clear day, you can see all the way to the Chesapeake Bay and to Virginia on the other side of it, right from our back porch. We sit in rocking chairs on the porch at night, to watch the sun go down. It's the most relaxing thing in the world.

When I'm down there, if I'm not riding my four-wheeler all over the place, I spend a lot of time working in the woods with my dad, or by myself. He used to work with his dad at their house in Beverly, Massachusetts. Once my parents bought Porto Bello, my dad would be out there every day with some project. I loved helping him, learning how to use a chain saw to clear brush and burn it. Still do. I love just being in the woods. It's so different from being in D.C.

Porto Bello, my favorite place in the world.

It's a really old place, so you can go on archae-ological digs all over the place. I find old arrow-heads and stuff all the time.

In general, I kind of think the place is haunted. So does my cousin Christopher, who comes to visit us there at Thanksgiving with the rest of my mom's family. He says he's scared shitless when he's there by himself. It's very quiet at night. But it can also get really windy, and when it does, it can be a bit scary. Someday I hope I'll live there. I'm going to have to get used to being there by myself first.

But when I was little, there with my parents, it was like paradise. We would go out there almost every weekend. And once I learned how to ride that four-wheeler, you pretty much had to pull me off of it. I take that thing all over the place, way back through the woods where there are barely even trails. (I've gotten stuck before, but I've learned how to avoid it.) When I'm riding through the woods on that four-wheeler, I feel like nothing can stop me. Close to nature, and in my own element. Nobody needs to tell me what to do—I just know. It's almost like surfing in that way.

One of the best things that ever happened to me was meeting Lisa Kelley in St. Mary's. She's my godmother now. Lisa is what I like to call a no-bullshit woman. She doesn't take any shit, and she doesn't give you any, either. Well, actually, she will give me shit, maybe a little. But I guess I deserve it sometimes.

Lisa, one of my true rocks and best friends, on my twenty-first birthday.

I met Lisa when I was thirteen, outside of Calvert Hall, on the campus of St. Mary's College. She was sitting on a bench. My parents had been giving me trouble about getting a job. I know it sounds weird, but I just walked right over to Lisa and said hi. Don't know what made me do it. The minute we made eye contact, we just bonded. I asked her for a job, and she said yes. She's been one of my best friends ever since.

Lisa and her husband, Michael, had moved down to St. Mary's from D.C. because they wanted to start their own family business. They had been working at one of the waterfront restaurants in D.C. and were looking for a change. They took over an old farmhouse in St. Mary's and turned it into a restaurant and inn, the Brome Howard. It's a great place. We go there for dinner all the time.

Working at the Brome Howard was my first job. I'd work on the weekends, during the day. I think my mom had told Lisa about my learning disabilities, because she was always incredibly patient with me. Lisa's son Dillon has what's called "fragile X," so I think she was better prepared than most to understand somebody like me. (Fragile X is a genetic syndrome that is more common in boys and involves pretty serious mental disabilities.)

At work I did whatever Lisa needed me to do. I didn't do an incredible amount, but it gave me something to do and kept me out of trouble. Not like I was a troubled kid or anything.

One of the reasons I loved working at the Brome Howard was because every day for lunch we ate barbecue sandwiches. They were so good. I'll never forget that, the big pot of pulled-pork barbecue. Another reason I loved the job was that I met my best friend, Stephen Ball, there.

We hit it off right away. Whenever I would come down to St. Mary's, Stephen and I would hang out, and he would introduce me to all of his friends. He was always there for me, if there was ever any trouble, and he showed me how to have a good time. When we were old enough, the two of us threw parties at Porto Bello.

Later, I went to high school at the Gow School, and Stephen went on to be a chef in the army for seven years, but we still saw each other whenever

My best friend, Stephen Ball.

we could. We were housemates in D.C. for about a year. A lot of people say that if you're best friends and you become housemates, that can completely end your relationship. But that hasn't been true with Stephen. He teases me about stuff that other people wouldn't be able to tease me about, and vice versa. He knows my struggles as well as anybody.

At the Brome Howard, I started off washing dishes in the basement. It was literally like a dungeon. It was really dark, and there was this huge sink that you had to push all these levers and stuff to use properly. It was pretty confusing for me at first, but eventually I figured it out.

You have to take orders on a job. I'd never really done that before. It's a good experience of how to deal with people. And you learn manners. If you're lucky, you can meet girls at work, too. I had some anxiety about the whole thing, just having to be outgoing and sociable and responsible for my job, but the truth is I liked that kind of work.

Spending all that time with Lisa really helped me, too. She was a little bit like a teacher. St. Mary's County, where the Brome Howard and Porto Bello are, is really like my second home now. And Lisa, she's the toughest woman in the world next to my mom. Ever since I've known her I've thought of her as kind of a second mother. And she has always treated me like her son.

Still, to this day, Lisa is one of my closest friends. I call her whenever I need advice, or if I need help.

Sometimes I just jump in the car and drive down to St. Mary's, because I miss her and want to see her. And she always makes room for me, even if I have to sleep on the couch. She gives me advice about girls, and tells me when I screw up. If I ever start complaining, Lisa will tell me to cut the bullshit. Sometimes you need to hear that from somebody other than a parent. I love her with all my heart, and always will. I have always thought she should run for president, if my mom doesn't first.

The Saga of Sparky Crowninshield Bradlee

When I was eleven, my grandmother had her first stroke. I never really got over it, the shock of seeing her like that. I spent a lot of time over at my grandparents' house. They were almost like my parents, but they treated me a little bit better. (My mother says, "That's the deal.") Nana spoiled me rotten, cooked me whatever I wanted, served me meals in bed. Good stuff. She's where I learned my "French," so to speak. She taught me how to swear. Dandy read me Bible stories a lot. And we were always playing Yankees and Rebels, Civil War games.

My mom's side of the family are Rebels, and my dad's side are Yankees. I'm half Northerner, half Southerner. My dad won't even go in the same room with grits. When I was a kid, particularly playing those games with my granddad, it was hard to know who was supposed to win. He had a picture of Robert E. Lee over his desk. In my heart, I always knew that the Yankees were right.

One day I was watching TV in the kitchen of my grandparents' house. My grandmother had a little office off of the kitchen. I could see her sitting on her chair, and then all of a sudden I saw her fall off of it. I'll never forget the sound of her hitting the floor. I went down in the elevator with her in the stretcher, and into the ambulance. I remember that day so clearly. I'll probably remember it for the rest of my life. I never saw Nana the same way again. She was almost okay after the first one, but she ended up having five strokes. By the last one, she was hardly even there anymore.

It was a bad time. My parents had heard that our friends Patience and Jim, who had a shih tzu named Poppy, were now giving away some of her litter of eight puppies. Patience and Jim's daughter, Lacie, is one of my oldest friends from growing up. Our moms basically went into labor together, and we've been two peas in a pod ever since.

With Lacie, one of my best and oldest friends.

(A lot of my friends growing up came through my parents like that. Patience and Jim were good friends of my parents, so I spent a lot of time with Lacie. Teddy Jones, another of my oldest and best friends growing up, was the son of Bo and Bebe Jones; Bo worked at the *Post* with my dad. When our parents would get together, the kids would all get together. Lacie and Teddy and Teddy's sister, Lindsay, are almost more like siblings than friends, because that's how much time we spent together.)

With Lindsay and Teddy Jones.

When my parents heard about the puppies, they decided that maybe that's what I needed to cheer up. We went over to look at the dogs on Christmas Eve. The hardest part about looking at a litter is that you feel bad, because you want to take them all home but you know you can't. Also, you don't want to separate them from their brothers and sisters and their mother. But eventually, dogs, like all other animals, they forget about their mother.

I started to look at the pups, and then I sat down on the couch to try to decide. There was one pup that they had named Hoppy, or at least I called him that, because he was born with only three and a half legs. I almost decided to bring him home with me, because I felt so bad for him.

But then all of a sudden this little black-and-white dog, I don't know how he did it, but he got enough strength in him to jump right up onto my lap and started licking my face. And that was pretty much that. He was so small I could hold him in one hand.

Sparky, the best dog there ever was.

They told me his name was Sparky. Lacie said that when she went to the vet to get him checked out, the vet asked what his name was and she just said "Sparky" without even really thinking about it. He was Sparky for the rest of his life. If you knew him, you could see that his name fit his personality perfectly. I remember trying to think of another name for him and I just couldn't do it. It was impossible.

They say dogs are man's best friend, and in my case it was true. Sparky was my best friend. As sad as it may sound, he was my only friend for a long time. I didn't have a lot of friends growing up. Not because I couldn't make them, but because I was always in the hospital. I was always seeing doctors. My difficulty with speech made it hard to communicate, and because everybody was so worried about my heart, there was a lot I couldn't do.

But Sparky was always there. Man, I loved that dog. For the first couple of days that we had him, he seemed really sad. My dad said, "Just talk to him." And I said, "You want me to talk to a dog?" But after a while, I did nothing but talk to him. They say that you end up looking like your dog, and your dog and you become one. I think it's true. I saw Sparky make some of the most human emotions. I even saw him cry a few times.

Once, we had a bad situation with a woman who worked for us in our house in Washington. Sparky knew something was wrong. One day my parents and I were standing in the kitchen, and Sparky was sitting in his bed under my mom's desk. My mom said, "Sparky, do you like this person?" And Sparky covered his eyes with his paws. He kind of rubbed his head and had his head under both of his paws for a minute. I knew that he was trying to tell us that something was wrong. You can believe that or not.

I wasn't always as nice to Sparky as I could have been. I played tricks on him sometimes. When you're eleven and you don't have any brothers or sisters around, you do some of the stuff that you would do to a brother or a sister with the dog. But Sparky never minded too much. Whenever I would come home from school, Sparky would already be at the door, wagging his tail. He knew it was me. There are scratch marks on the door from Sparky that we've never painted over. I just wanted to leave them there. When he died of old age two years ago, I buried his ashes in the cemetery at Porto Bello, so he could always be there with us.

I spent a lot of time alone as a kid, and Sparky was always there for me. When you don't have a lot of friends, and you're in the doctor's office a lot of the time, that's really all you've got. He loved going to the farm, and chasing rabbits, and being our watchdog. I recommend that anybody like me get a dog. They are a lot of work, but then so is life.

When I was feeling down, I could just watch Sparky chasing his tail around and around. At first I thought that was just a Sparky thing, but later I found out it's a dog thing. One time watching him, I literally fell down laughing. Those are good things to remember.

Sparky Crowninshield Bradlee

The
Discovery

The list of unexplained medical complications I had continued until I was about fourteen. When I was thirteen, I developed a ringing in my ears, which is called tinnitus. (I still have it today.) I also developed a small bone growth on my jaw. Nobody could explain where any of it was coming from.

When I was fourteen, I developed a really, really scratchy throat. All Bradlee men have scratchy voices, so we didn't really think anything of it. But it wouldn't go away, and it kind of hurt.

Eventually I went back to the hospital, the ole home away from home, for some tests. They found out that one of my vocal cords was paralyzed. Just another thing to add to the list.

The doctors didn't know what was happening. This is from the doctor who diagnosed me:

It is my impression that Quinn Bradlee is a 14 year old young man who has an apparent new onset of a left vocal cord paralysis. . . . When all is said and done, I am not sure that we are going to come to a specific diagnosis of Quinn's condition. Isolated vocal cord paralysis has been reported as a viral or post viral syndrome. Only time will tell if this is the correct diagnosis, and usually such a diagnosis is one of exclusion.

In other words, we don't know shit.

At the time, it seemed like each of my doctors had a different opinion. And with each new opinion, my parents were given a new theory on why I was the way I was. Another doctor who saw me at the time described me this way:

His vocal cord paralysis cannot be explained by his past surgery for congenital heart disease. . . . I have discussed with the mother Josiah's learning disabilities. She has been told that this is due to a lack of oxygen during the time of his ventricular septal defect repair [the surgery when I was three months old]. This is not the case, since he was repaired while on cardiac bypass without circulatory arrest. Children undergoing cardiac bypass may have mild disabilities as a result but typically these do not have a dramatic impact on their subsequent development.

I couldn't really tell you what half of that means, but you can tell that they couldn't figure out what was wrong with me. There was some link, but nobody knew what it was.

They tested me for a week to try to figure out my vocal-cord issue. They thought it might be cancer for a while, which of course thrilled my mom. X-rays, CAT scans, sonograms, a whole week. Everything negative.

In desperation, my mom went to the speech therapist at Children's Hospital to ask if there was anything else she could think of. The woman called a friend of hers at the National Institutes of Health, who started asking all these questions about me. At the end she said, "You know, this sounds like Shprintzen syndrome." (That's what VCFS is sometimes called, because Dr. Robert Shprintzen discovered it.)

Nobody at Children's Hospital had ever heard of Shprintzen's syndrome. I'd been treated there for fourteen years, but nobody had any idea. The woman at NIH said, "You should go see Dr. Shprintzen." At that time he was at Montefiore Hospital, in New York City. Over that summer, we went to visit him.

When we walked into Dr. Shprintzen's office, he took one look at me and said, "Yup, he's got it." The rest of my life changed from there.

Dr. Shprintzen and VCFS

Dr. Shprintzen can tell you about VCFS and about how he figured it all out a lot better than I can. We interviewed him for a movie that I made, and later for this book. It wouldn't make sense for me to pretend to tell you everything that he knows as if I know it, too. Nobody would believe it anyway. So I asked him if we could use his words to explain VCFS, how he discovered it and everything, and he said yes. So here they are.

Dr. Shprintzen

The study of human genetics is a relatively new field in medicine. I started professionally back in 1973, running a cranio-facial center, when the scientific study of cleft lip and cleft palate was just really getting under way. My training was in speech disorders, speech physiology, but I sat at the head of a multi-disciplinary center, so I became more knowledgeable about a lot of different fields.

One day I got a call from somebody asking if I wanted to hire a genetic counselor, and I didn't even know what that was. So I asked the age-old question, "All right, how much is it going to cost me?" And they said, "Nothing." So I said, "Okay, then I'll take two." So I took on some students in genetic counseling.

It became apparent to me right at the outset that this was going to be interesting in terms of the patients I was seeing at the time, many of whom had multiple congenital anomalies and clearly some kind of genetic-based disorder. We just didn't know what it was, because the profession was in its infancy. There really was no specific training in clinical genetics at the time, so I found doctors here and there who could help me. There was no formal way to prepare. And the laboratory techniques available were so primitive compared with what we have today. Back then we knew of hundreds of genetic diseases; now the NIH has classified more than 18,000.

Within a span of just a few months, I saw maybe a half a dozen kids, relatively close together, who looked similar, who all had congenital heart disease, and who were all referred in because they either had a cleft palate or they had severely abnormal speech. They all had a history of learning disabilities and congenital heart disease. It became apparent to me that there was a pattern here, and it didn't fit anything else that had been reported before. This was by 1975. Over the next year I saw another half dozen cases, and there was clearly something here that was different.

We published our first paper about it in 1978, naming it velo-cardio-facial syndrome. "Velo" stands for velum, and it's the Latin term for the soft palate. "Cardio" obviously for heart defects, and "Facial" because of the charac-

Dr. Robert Shprintzen, the man who got
it right.

*teristic facial appearance. Not an abnormal one, just a
characteristic one. The most common findings associated
with the syndrome are congenital heart diseases, which we
see in about 70 percent of patients; palate and speech problems, which we see in about 75 percent of cases; vascular
problems of one type or another in nearly all cases; and either some type of learning disability or even some psychiatric
problems in nearly all cases as well.*

*We eventually figured out, through collaboration with
other scientists, that the cause of VCFS was what's called*

a submicroscopic deletion of a small segment of DNA on chromosome 22. It happens randomly, in an instant, during DNA recombination in reproductive cell formation, and we have no ability to reconstruct it experimentally. It just happens. It has nothing to do with a parent's age, lifestyle, or anything like that. But once the syndrome is present in somebody, it is inherited as an autosomal dominant trait—which means that the risk for having a child with VCFS, if you have VCFS, is fifty percent, or about the same as flipping a coin.

Over time, we've discovered more than 180 different characteristics that are associated with the syndrome, everything from the most common characteristics to things like hypocalcemia in infancy (a deficiency in calcium metabolism that can result in seizures) to scoliosis, immune disorders, a different growth and development pattern, and the appearance of tapered fingers in many patients. Research has also shown that the deletion of this part of the genome makes one more susceptible to schizophrenia and other psychiatric conditions.

In general, we're still working on trying to figure out why some kids get very extreme cases, while others are so mild as to be undetectable. In genetics, we call this "variable expression," because the same set of genetic circumstances leads to different results in different people. Same thing as when my brother and I got the same strand of chicken pox, and he was fine in two days and I ended up with pox all over the place and a wicked ear infection.

Because we have so many different findings in the syndrome, there's more than one treatment. Very often, we're treating individual components of the disorder. So, for example, with congenital heart disease, we're dealing with a surgical procedure. For speech problems, we're dealing with a combination of surgery and speech therapy. For some of the psychiatric issues, then we're dealing with medications. The learning disorders require special educational strategies and sometimes the medical management of ADHD.

"Cure" is an interesting word. The question is, once a child is born with the syndrome, can we treat everything associated with it in an effective way, so that people lead a perfectly normal life? And I do believe that's largely possible, in most cases.

*   *   *

When I first met Quinn, I knew that he had VCFS just because I've seen so many patients that I've kind of got the feel for it now. I think we could all agree objectively that Quinn is a good-looking kid. He's really a very attractive young man. So the issue isn't that people with VCFS look abnormal, because they don't. It's just that they all tend to resemble each other, in some ways, more than they resemble their own families. Quinn's appearance was fairly typical of VCFS. But if a regular guy saw Quinn walking down the street and didn't know who he was, he'd never have any idea.

Generally, though, Quinn is on the milder end of the expression, and that's clearly one of the reasons why he came to the diagnosis pretty late in life. If he'd had more obvious manifestations, I think that the diagnosis might have been made earlier. It's hard to know. Sometimes you just have to run across the right professional.

That said, Quinn's speech problem was pretty significant at the time. He wasn't real happy about it, nor were his folks. Because the syndrome has such specific findings in how the throat muscles function or don't function, it was really important that we were able to identify the syndrome—but also to identify the exact lack of muscle movement that required reconstructions.

It turned out that Quinn required a pharyngeal flap operation, even though he'd already had a few. Pharyngeal flap surgery is a reconstruction of the back of the throat, so that if too much air is escaping through the nose during speech, we can lock it effectively and normalize the speech pattern, the resonance. If there are articulation problems and other speech problems, we treat those with speech therapy.

In that first meeting, we also made a smaller but perhaps even more critical diagnosis. Quinn's parents told me that they'd noticed huge mood swings in Quinn right before I first saw him. Big depressions, then some screaming and yelling—generally acting out and not in control of his emotions. I asked them if he was on any medications, and Sally told me that he had been on Ritalin for years, to help him with his ADD [attention deficit disorder] in school. We took him off of it immediately. Some VCFS kids can't handle Ritalin. (Ritalin can be effective in childhood for maintaining attention, but it can contribute to agitation and mood disorders because of an elevation of certain brain chemicals that are controlled by genes in the deleted region of chromosome 22.) This is the kind of expertise that we've developed over time, and why sometimes it can be a relief for families to finally get the diagnosis. In a small way, they can know what they're dealing with. Sally reported that within two days, Quinn was back to being himself.

We're really good at fixing the physical problem. Our success rate there is really high. But in issues of learning and education, it's not as surefire at all.

After the Diagnosis

When I interviewed my mom for the documentary I made about VCFS two years ago, she said, "A lot of people are devastated when you find out your child has some syndrome that's serious. I was enormously relieved, because it explained everything to me. All of the terrible things that had been happening to Quinn since he was born, suddenly there was an explanation."

I tend to think that my diagnosis was a bigger deal for my parents than it was for me. When there is something "wrong" with your child, parents often feel responsible. I guess technically you *are* responsible, because you decided to have the kid, but you know what I mean. My mom and dad were old when they had me. My dad was sixty, and my mom was forty-one. I think they thought that might be a factor in how I turned out. In that way the diagnosis was a relief, because their age had nothing to do with my trouble. VCFS is the result of a random genetic combination during reproduction. The biggest

relief is that every time a problem comes up, now
my mom can call Shprintzen and say, "Is this part of
the package?"

But for me, nothing really changed after the diagnosis. It was just the luck of the draw. But I did
have the pharyngeal flap surgery, which helped me
talk better. Before I knew I had VCFS, when things
were bad with my health or at school, I didn't go
around all the time thinking, "Oh, I'm learning disabled," or, "There's something wrong with me."

All of my life I had been in schools where kids
learned the way I did. I only encountered a few
people who, when I asked them for something, just
looked at me like I was from Mars, like I had these
big tentacles on my head or something. Being sick
all the time and going to the Lab School and all, I
just thought that was normal. I really did.

When we got the diagnosis, I was confused. My
parents were relieved, because now they had something they could say. I wasn't sure whether it was
good news or bad news. I didn't know whether to be
satisfied or not. With my diagnosis, nothing changed,
and everything changed. But I didn't start blaming
everything I did wrong on that. I thought, "All right,
well now I know I have VCFS and that's responsible
for a lot of my trouble with my health and in school.
But what can I really blame on it? I'm still the same
person."

And the truth is, even now I really don't think
about it all that much. If you think about how shitty
the world is going to be, or is now, you're just going

to be depressed. I'm not saying VCFS is the end of the world. I'm just saying, if you concentrate on something that you perceive as difficult or bad, you're just going to be more depressed. And I just kind of learned to cope with that. This is who I am. So be it.

The biggest question a diagnosis like mine leaves you with is, "What's normal, and what's VCFS?" It was nice to know that the difficulties I'd had were all part of a larger syndrome, but there was no real road map of what was "normal" and what was a result of my having VCFS. And I couldn't call Dr. Shprintzen every time I wanted an answer. Even today, when I'm doing something, sometimes I think, "Is this normal for me to do? Is this not normal?" When you have a syndrome that nobody's ever heard of, there are a lot of times when you don't know if what you're doing is normal, if everybody else does it, or if you're doing something wrong.

Because nobody really knows what VCFS is, it's hard to know what to say when people ask about it. That's why I always say I'm dyslexic, even though that's not the full story. When people ask what VCFS is, the explanation takes so long that I want to say, "I don't know, dude. It's a disorder." But you can't do that. Most people I've explained VCFS to are very understanding, but if I get lost in the middle of nowhere, I never go up to somebody and say, "I'm lost and I have VCFS." They'd look at me like I was from Mars. I hope maybe this book will help change that.

Transition into High School

My dad went away to boarding school, and his dad went away to boarding school, and so in a way I kind of felt like I *should* go away to boarding school. I joke that it was more that my parents wanted to get rid of me, but it was my choice. I thought it was really the only option I had for getting a good education. The Lab School had been great, but I'd been there since I was four, and I think my whole family felt like it was time for a change.

Along with deciding to go to boarding school, it was around this time that I got my driver's license. (The psychologist who said I would never drive was wrong.) I had to study constantly to prepare for the written part of the driving test. My mom drilled me on it all the time. When I went to take the test, a friend of mine who ended up going to Harvard was there with me. I passed with a higher score. I was pretty proud of that. And I could drive. (I failed the driving exam three times, but I finally passed.)

I went to look at boarding schools with my parents. When we arrived at the very first one, Gow,
I just knew I wanted to go. My dad went to St.
Mark's, an all-boys prep school, and this was the
closest thing I'd ever seen to that. I wanted to be like
my dad. And also, it was beautiful. My mom remembers me saying, "This is my place." I don't remember
that, but I did know that it was a hard school to get
into, and that I'd be lucky to get in.

The people at the Lab School thought it was a
real stretch for me, and that if I did get in that it
would be a serious challenge. Gow specializes in
kids with dyslexia and learning disabilities, and it's
in a little town called New South Wales, New York,
near Buffalo. There are a lot of schools now that are
for kids with learning disabilities, but Gow was one
of the first. It's definitely one of the hardest, or at
least that's what it seemed like at the time.

I did end up getting in. I'm not sure my mom
was as happy about the news as I was. The weekend
we found out, we were up in Boston and my mom
was so freaked out about the separation boarding
school would cause that she thought she was having
a heart attack. We'd never been away from each
other for more than a few weeks. My dad flagged
down an ambulance and we went to the hospital. It
turned out my mom was just suffering from anxiety
about the whole thing. She can be a little high-
strung at times.

Gow ended up being really good and really bad
for me at the same time. The best part is that I got

With my parents at Gow, a new chapter.

in, and I graduated on the Dean's List. It's kind of like, "Take that," you know?

The good parts were largely academic. Gow gave me the best education I could have gotten. It was hard, but I loved the academic aspect of it. And good experiences for kids with learning disabilities can be hard to come by.

One of the best things at Gow was the typing class they made us take. The teacher would put this special thing over the keyboard with enough room for your hands, but you couldn't see your hands or where the keys were. I hated every minute of it. But at the end, I was typing forty words per minute, and it changed my life.

My dad tells me how he'd wished he'd learned how to type like that, because he still types with finger pokes. In high school and college, being able to type saves your ass. Your neck sure appreciates it, too. When you have to keep looking up and down it's what I like to call computer head-banging.

My two favorite subjects at Gow were English and Reconstructive Language, a course in the roots of language. You don't learn all of Latin and Greek, but you do learn what suffixes and prefixes mean, so you can understand words better.

In English class, we read Shakespeare. Because it was hard for most of us to follow, we read a lot of the plays in class. One kid would read, or we would all take turns playing the roles. We read *Macbeth* and *Othello*. I especially liked *Macbeth* because of my Scottish ancestry. I think we all kind of wish we had royal blood in us. Sometimes when they would say "Macbeth," I would imagine that they were saying my name instead. It was a cool way to read Shakespeare.

I don't remember *Othello* that well, but I do remember Iago. At one point he says, "I am not what I am." I wrote that down in my journal. I think most LD kids could relate to that. It also made me understand why my parents say that not every writer can be as good as Shakespeare, not even them.

My favorite memory from Gow is from my freshman year. I was struggling a lot with math, and I called home in tears one night because I was so far behind. And I was only taking pre-algebra, so I was already behind, because most freshmen at Gow were taking algebra. My teacher, Jeff Sweet, called my parents at the beginning of the year and told my mom that there are people who understand math and there are people who don't, and that I was one of those people who just didn't get it. We'd just have to work around it.

My mom tried to cheer me up by saying that she basically failed math and that it means nothing to most people. But the trouble is that I wanted to be good at it and understand it.

There are times when you look at a math problem, and you just say, "No way. There's no way I can solve this." But my teacher taught me that before you say "No way," you should just look at it and see if there is anything you *can* do. At one point I was given a really tough problem in that algebra class. I said, "No way." But Jeff Sweet told me to go back and look at it. It turned out to be pretty easy once I started. Your eyes and mind differentiate what they see. It's like when some things smell really bad, but they taste good.

Toward the middle of the year, I don't know what happened but all of a sudden I just understood algebra. I was doing extra math problems, trying to teach myself geometry, and I started to get A's and B's. On one test toward the end of the year, there was a problem that nobody else got but me. Mr. Sweet asked, "How'd you do that?" I didn't know. It finally just made sense to me.

At the end of the year, Gow gives out a number of awards. When they got to the math awards, I had a feeling that it was going to be me. It was pretty amazing. When they called my name, you should have seen my parents. I'm pretty sure I'm the only one in my family to ever receive a math award.

That was one of the best experiences I ever had at school. It's one of the few really good memories that I have of any school. I can't do math to save my ass now, but that isn't the point. The point is that there were teachers calling my parents and telling them I wasn't going to make it. And there were doctors who told my parents I would never have any friends, never be able to read or write, never play sports, never be able to graduate from high school or college.

I graduated from high school with honors, and I won the Browning Award three times for being a good student and being interested in continuing my studies. What I would like to tell all the people who discouraged me is not, as they say, fit to print. Sometimes nobody thought I could do it, even me. And then I did it anyway.

The
Hard Parts

———

The worst part of Gow was that there were no girls. Just a bunch of learning-disabled dudes who have to wear coats and ties every day, in the middle of nowhere. How fun is that? Gow was founded in 1926, and the only thing that hasn't changed is that it's still all boys. After my experience there, I believe that it's the school's biggest flaw.

Socially, Gow was really hard for me. It was my first time living away from home. I struggled a lot with that at first. I'd been to overnight camps prior to Gow, but leaving home—really leaving home for the first time—can be scary. You're going to a place where you've never been and that you know nothing about. I knew it was going to be tough and not just a walk in the park, because school never is.

More important, it was my first time really being surrounded by people my age. I'm an only child. I have two half brothers and a half sister, and I love them all a lot, but they're a lot older than I am and I didn't really grow up with them. I grew up with my parents and their friends. Their friends were kind of my friends. I was very, very used to adults. I didn't grow up like a regular kid in that way.

I knew the language adults spoke better than the language of people my age. I heard the expression "sick" for the first time at Gow. You know, like "That's a sick car you have there," or something. I was working on a project, and somebody said, "That drawing's pretty sick," and I thought he was making fun of me. I asked what the hell he was talking about, and I got all upset about it. I kind of got into a verbal fight with these kids, before they told me "sick" was a compliment. Stuff like that happened to me a lot.

It's kind of like learning surfer language. Surf jargon, nobody understands but surfers. I had to adapt when I got to Gow. Anybody can adapt to something, but it just takes a lot longer for some people.

I had a hard time making friends. I made some mistakes at first and I think they kind of screwed me for the whole time I was at Gow. Sometimes when I felt insecure about something, or if I didn't know what to say, I would brag a little bit about my family. At the time I didn't even think I was bragging. I didn't have the greatest social skills, so if somebody mentioned World War II or something I would talk about my granddad, Buffalo Bill. I thought I was making simple conversation. But in the end, it kicked me in the ass, and ever since then I've just kind of kept it to myself.

Once everybody found out who my parents were, it ruined things for me at Gow. Some kids were jealous. Other kids kind of used me. I didn't really know how to make friends, so when people would ask to borrow things—money, DVDs, calling cards— I would give them what they wanted, because I wanted to have friends. Often the people who borrowed things didn't return them, or ended up bad-mouthing me for what I thought was just being a nice guy.

Gow was just sort of a tough place. A lot of kids ran around hazing each other. The reasons may never be determined, but sometimes it can just be out of pure boredom, which is sad but true. Boys can be very aggressive, but I think they are even more so when they are together, without a woman in sight. If a beautiful girl had walked by while we were fighting, I think we would have gotten distracted. Like everybody, I used to get teased, but that's something that every kid has to prepare himself for, no matter how cool they think they are. I don't think it was because I had VCFS or anything. It was just regular boarding-school hazing, with the special twist that these were kids who felt different anyway and so maybe were even a bit wilder.

Sometimes it could be brutal. One kid who had a growth problem—he was hip height—got locked in a locker for a couple of hours by a bunch of kids. Other kids would come up and punch you for no reason. There was just a lot of testosterone in the air.

I didn't get the worst of it, but that kind of hazing happened all the time, to almost everybody. You didn't live in fear or anything, but it was always present, very much *Lord of the Flies* territory. When one of the dorm masters (a guy who was there when I was there) left, he said it was because of how crazy the kids were.

Roommates

My freshman- and sophomore-year roommates were okay. You can pick your roommates once you've been there for a while, but as I said I had a hard time making friends. Nobody ever really wanted to be my roommate. So I'd always be one of the left-out kids who got randomly picked after everybody else had decided who they wanted to live with.

My sophomore year, this kid Andrew and I realized that nobody wanted to room with either of us. We asked ourselves, "Why don't we room together?" At least we knew each other, and we wouldn't be stuck with some jerk. Andrew was a super-tall, really nice guy. Living with him worked out pretty well. I wonder where he is now.

During my junior year I had two different roommates. The first had pierced nipples, and it turned out that he was the biggest drug lord on campus. We had really shallow closets, just deep enough for our coats and jackets and ties. My roommate had a pile of laundry that he kept on stacking and stacking and stacking, until finally our dorm master came in and pushed it over. Two big bricks of marijuana were sitting right there, under all the dirty clothes. The headmaster kicked something like fifteen kids out of school that day, mostly A and B students, and my roommate was one of them.

So I got a new roommate. I liked him at first. He seemed like a really cool guy. He was from Georgia, and my mom's from Georgia, so we at least had a little in common.

But before long he started doing all kinds of weird shit. He would lock me out of the room and then demand a different password each time I got back from the bathroom, in order to get back in. Sometimes I'd be dripping wet, just out of the shower. I didn't want to be a tattletale, really. When you're in high school, you don't really know how to handle that sort of situation. I didn't, at least.

Right before Christmas, I'd gotten some shopping money for Christmas presents. I told my roommate about it, but didn't make a big deal of it. When I woke up the next morning, the whole side of my room was turned upside down. All the drawers were open, all my stuff was on the floor. And $250 was stolen right out of my wallet.

At that time, I wasn't smart enough to think that maybe it was my new roommate who was responsible. I hadn't been in a lot of living situations and didn't have a lot of experience with kids, so I didn't think, "Well, it's probably him." He started acting, going along with me, trying to figure out who stole my money.

Then it got weirder. One day one of the teaching assistants came into our room to check on us, a guy I liked named Steve. He was from the Dominican Republic, and he had dark skin. My roommate started calling him the N-word and cursing at him. The TA didn't really do anything, and neither did my roommate—it was just name-calling. But it made me really uncomfortable.

There was a Jewish kid on campus who always wore a yarmulke. Not long after the incident with the TA, my roommate threatened him, putting a knife to his throat. After that, my roommate was kicked out right away. In one year I'd lived with a drug dealer and a neo-Nazi racist. Not all that sweet.

Gow was a tough school. Nobody really knows all that went on there. There was a lot of bullying. There were a lot of times where the teachers didn't believe what was happening around them.

I really enjoyed my Reconstructive Language class. The teacher was a really nice guy, and I looked forward to seeing him every day. But in the class there was a kid named Bobo, who was a real jerk. If you asked a stupid question, he would kick you. Sometimes the teacher would *tell* him to kick you. One day, after I asked what I thought was a pretty reasonable question, the teacher told Bobo to kick me. And it wasn't just me—he did it to other people, too. I ended up being a little scared to go to that class. Might I remind readers that all of this was happening at a school for kids with dyslexia and learning problems, who need a little more understanding than other kids?

At Gow, kids hit each other all the time. I hated it. If you said something stupid, you often got hit. But everybody says stupid stuff. I think those kids were afraid of being dyslexic. Hitting someone or name-calling maybe made them feel better about their own situation. But I guess also, if you put a bunch of rowdy kids together with no girls in the middle of nowhere, where it snows thirty inches in two nights and it's –25 degrees, what else are they going to do? Kick the shit out of each other.

The sad thing about kids who get teased the way I did is that they aren't always taken seriously when they go for help. There was a story in the *New York Times* recently about a kid in Arkansas who was getting bullied all the time, but nobody at the school would help him. I understood his situation completely. Nobody believed him, but he was obviously right. And they held it against him that he tried to stand up for himself every once in a while. Not being taken seriously can lead a person to feel depressed, suicidal even. I wish they had video cameras everywhere in high schools. That way, people would be forced to believe some of the awful stuff that goes on behind closed doors.

If the teachers wouldn't help me, sometimes I would end up calling my mom. I know they some-

times didn't like it at the school. But they weren't doing shit. When I called my mom, she got results.
And as she would say, I'm a very results-oriented
person. I think maybe I get it from my grandfather,
who was an intelligence officer and a soldier. He
liked results, too.

St. Martin

I had what you might call an "extra-curricular" experience during my time at Gow, when I took a vacation with my family to St. Martin.

My parents used to go to the same place in the Caribbean every year, to a hotel called La Samanna in St. Martin. It's right on the water and has its own beach. Once I was old enough, I could choose a companion to help keep me company during those trips. When I was nineteen, I decided to bring a guy I knew from Gow. Though I had a hard time making friends at Gow, this kid had always been nice to me, and I thought he'd have fun in St. Martin with me. Maybe it would bring us closer.

Like everyone in the world, he knew that I wanted to get laid and that I'd had a difficult time with that. The first thing he said to me before we left was, "I'm gonna get you laid."

The third night that we were on the island, we hired a taxi to take us out on the town. My mom being who she is, she asked the hotel for the most reputable driver they knew. She told the managers of the hotel that she wanted somebody to take us to bars where kids hung out, to wait for us, and to take us back to the hotel at the end of the night.

The driver was named Silky. He was a bald islander who wore a hat and lots of gold jewelry. When he asked where we wanted to go, my friend said, "Just take us to some bars." In hindsight, I think maybe my friend talked to him before I got there.

St. Martin is divided into two sides, the French side and the Dutch side. I think the French side is nicer and had assumed we were going out on the French side, but it turned out that we were heading to the Dutch side. To me, it kind of looked like a Third World country.

After driving for about half an hour, we pulled up to what looked like a bar. We were the only white people in the entire place, and I felt a little uncomfortable. The bar was called Heaven's Gate. I had no idea what Heaven's Gate referred to. I hadn't been introduced to that world yet, if you know what I mean.

I realized pretty quick that every guy in the bar was talking to a girl, and every girl was sitting in a guy's lap in a very sexual way. After we both got beers, my friend disappeared. So I found an empty seat and sat down.

The next thing I knew, a girl had come over to me and sat down on my lap, just like that. She had skin that was as dark as the night sky and black curly hair that came down to her shoulders. She sat there, and I very nervously and slowly put both of my arms around her waist. I had no idea what to do.

She stood up, took my hand, and led me to a paying stand. It looked very much like a booth where you would buy tickets for a play. "It" only cost $35. That night, I only had about that much. Maybe it was destiny.

After I paid, she took me down a very narrow hall with red doors on each side, and then into one of the rooms. I was still a little confused about what was happening. When she started to take off her clothes, I finally realized what was going on. Once she got on the bed, I immediately and nervously took off all my clothes, too.

You can guess what happened next. I don't need to go into too much detail. I'm glad that it happened, I guess, but it wasn't necessarily the way that I wanted to lose my virginity. I might have bragged a little about just wanting to get laid, but in reality I wanted to lose my virginity with somebody I really cared about and who cared about me. I didn't really know what was going on that night, for the most part. But the one thing I understood afterwards was the pure satisfaction possible when you make love to somebody you are truly in love with.

When I woke up the next day, the first thing that came into my mind was, "How am I going to tell my parents?" You might wonder why I wanted to do that, but at that time in my life, I was really used to telling them everything. (I still do tell them just about everything, to be honest.) They were my best friends. And so I was confused. I wanted to tell them what had happened, but I didn't exactly know how to. I thought if I did, I better tell my father before my mother.

When I walked out onto the terrace, my dad was there, reading the newspaper as he does every morning. He gets really into it and doesn't like being interrupted. But this time I figured he might like to hear what just happened to his youngest son.

Before I sat down, I said to him, "Guess what, Dad?" "What?" he asked. I didn't know any other way to say it, so I just told him, "I got laid." All he asked was, "How'd it feel?" My dad being who he is, I figured he'd say a lot more than that, but I was wrong. I didn't have much to say about it, but I think my dad was happy for me.

All of a sudden, my mother walked out onto the terrace. I don't know if she heard what I said or what, but it was weird that she walked in right as we were talking about it. She asked what was going on, and I told her the whole story.

All hell broke loose.

My mother worries way too much, if you ask me. I know that mothers worry; all mothers do and they're supposed to. But she took this one a little far.

The first thing she did was ask me if I was joking. I think she was so stunned that she didn't believe me. The next thing she asked was whether I'd used a condom or not, which of course I had. When she found out that I'd lost my virginity at a "house of ill repute," she went nuts.

The only thing that my mom was thinking about was whether I could have gotten HIV. The year before, when we were in St. Martin, I had had a terrible migraine and ended up spending the night in an HIV ward in a hospital on the French side of the island. I had forgotten about it, but my mom hadn't. She started to go on and on about how many people on the island had AIDS. She was making me upset, but she was making herself even more upset.

At this point my friend came in, and I explained that I'd told my mother, thinking that she would be proud of me. My friend couldn't believe that I told her. I guess he didn't realize how much I confided in my mom. Maybe I confided in her more than I should have. Knowing what I know now, I probably would have told Lisa instead of my mom. But the fact is that I've always told my parents the truth. My mom says that she's never caught me in a lie in my life. I just don't believe in lying.

My mother started to call every doctor she knew to tell them what happened. My dad calls it "going to General Quarters," from the navy. It means getting the ship ready for battle, and boy, was my mom on the warpath. She took us to the front desk of the hotel, where she gave them a talking to. The hotel called Silky, who took all of us back down to Heaven's Gate.

The manager of Heaven's Gate was an elegantly dressed woman, which I thought was surprising. Her office looked like the inside of IBM or something—very professional. My mom was relieved to find out that it was a medically inspected place used mostly by government officials.

The manager was very cooperative and understanding. She could see that my mom was panicked. My mom asked her to find the girls we had been with. It took them about half an hour to find them. While we were waiting for the girls to come back, not one word was spoken. It was the only time in my life that I've been too afraid to talk to my mother.

When the girls showed up, I was more relieved than scared or nervous. They got in the car with us, and Silky took us all to the clinic for an HIV test. Talk about awkward. My mom and dad sat in the front with Silky, and we sat in back with the girls. (They ended up being clean, thank God. They were also very nice about the whole thing, though since they didn't speak much English, I'm not sure I really knew how they were feeling. Confused, probably.)

I don't think my mother was intentionally trying to embarrass me, but I had never been embarrassed like that before. I couldn't wait to leave St. Martin. I have never wanted to leave any place like I did that day. I learned two things from the experience: My father was much of more of a ladies' man when he was my age than I am now, and also never to upset my mother.

When my friend and I got back to Gow, we both kind of went our own way. But then kids randomly started coming up to me and asking how my vacation was in a suggestive way. The infamous Bobo was telling people that I had slept with a hooker. I told Bobo that my friend was guilty of the same charge, but Bobo told everybody that only I had done it, and not my friend.

If I didn't know what humiliation was before that moment, I sure felt it then. It ruined my last couple of months at Gow, because people were constantly making jokes about me and the hooker. I'm a sensitive person, so the jokes hurt—even if people were just kidding. And I thought that the kid who had been with me in St. Martin was spreading lies, too. I didn't think that I would ever be able to forgive him.

Recently, I saw his profile on Facebook, and I wrote him to say that I was going to be telling this story in my book. He said that he had never told lies about me, that he wished we were still friends, and that Bobo had spread all the stories. Whatever happened, it was one of the hardest times of my life.

End on a
Positive Note

———

So Gow was really up and down for me, socially in particular. I absolutely loved the academics but had a hard time with the other kids. I decided to stick it out, because I knew what a great education I was getting. When my mom asked me if I wanted to transfer after my second year at Gow, I said no. I knew it was good for me.

If there was anything that saved me at Gow, it was poetry. When we started studying e. e. cummings and William Butler Yeats, reading their work really got me into writing. A lot of people like e. e. cummings because he was the first guy who basically said, look, you can do what you want when you write. Just look at his name. You can write whatever you want. You don't have to use the right punctuation or capitalization or any of that stuff. You can do it the way that comes naturally to you.

For kids with reading problems, cummings' poems can give you courage and motivation. I'm not saying you want to give learning-disabled kids license to write like him all the time. But the beauty of poetry is that you can write however you want to write. It doesn't matter. Discovering that was really exciting to me.

Jamie Perry was the best English teacher I had. He introduced me to poetry my sophomore year at Gow. He was great. He would show us clips from movies of the books we were reading. At Gow, the teachers try to offer visual examples, because they know that it's often the easiest way for learning-disabled kids to learn.

After Perry's class, I started writing poetry all the time, much of it about Ireland. It was all I wanted to talk about. Ireland this, Ireland that. (I'm still fascinated with Ireland, because most of my mom's side of the family started off there.) I think writing poetry really helped me get through school. It was a way to get my feelings out, almost as if I was talking to somebody.

I still have the books I wrote the poems in, but I'm not dumb enough to put them in here. Poetry by sixteen-year-old kids sucks by definition. Maybe even if you're Shakespeare.

Testing

When I look back at what worked and what didn't work for me in school, it's hard for me to remember. I do know that standardized testing is not really my thing. The SATs pretty much handed me my ass. They made me realize the kind of difficulty I'm up against because of my learning disabilities.

We interviewed Mark Szafnicki, one of my Reconstructive Language teachers from Gow, to illustrate an instance when I had trouble, so I could understand it. And of course, Dr. Shprintzen has his ideas about my difficulties, too. I hope their words will help you understand what I was up against.

Mark Szafnicki
Quinn is a good phonetic reader, or someone who reads and uses good intonation. You wouldn't know that he's having trouble reading by listening to him read. It's when you ask him questions about what he's read that there are gaps. He

certainly made improvement on his understanding over the course of the year that I had with him.

In the class he was in, he had good relationships with his peers. Most of the other boys in the class were kids who had more trouble phonetically reading, and didn't have as good intonation as Quinn did. They had more difficulty reading orally, but maybe had a better understanding of what they were reading than Quinn did. There was some give and take, and nobody felt superior to anyone else in the class.

We were reading a story about a man and his two children, and he was teaching them to sail. They used the term "knockabout" in the story. I could tell whoever was reading, there was a loss of comprehension there. I stopped the class, and I said, "Who knows what a knockabout is?" There was evidence within the story that you might be able to figure it out based on the context, but Quinn piped up right away, from his experience. I don't necessarily think that he got anything from the context, but from his experience he said, "It's a type of boat. It's like a sailboat." Everybody was like, "Oh, okay. All right." So it made the story. It made perfect sense.

They went on reading the story, and that day for home-work I gave homework of about five questions. They were multiple choices. One of the questions was, "What's a knockabout?" Quinn was the only student in the class to get the answer wrong. When we were going over the ques-tions the next day, I said, "Well, who got this one wrong?" and Quinn raised his hand. Another student just kind of did a double take, and said, "Quinn, how on earth did you get that wrong? I got that question right because you told us the answer!" Quinn was like, "Oh, yeah."

It was just that there was that lapse of comprehension. I still often think of that, and think, "Why didn't Quinn get that right?" I'm not sure I know the answer. When I asked the question orally, "What's a knockabout?" Quinn had an answer orally, but when the question was in writing and he had to read it for himself, for some reason the connection was totally different or there was no connection. He processed what I said and had the answer, but with the same question on paper, for some reason he didn't make the connection. He was the only one, and everyone else in the class credited their getting the answer right to Quinn. And he didn't get it right.

I think part of him was confused, and part of him was surprised. I think he just came to a realization, and said, "Yeah. I guess I should have gotten that. I don't know why I didn't." So it was confusion, but I never saw any embarrassment. He doesn't get frustrated, because he can read the words. But there is just sometimes a blankness there when you talk about the meaning of what he's reading. Like there is this blank space between us, and neither of us can penetrate it to get to the other side. We can kind of see each other behind it, but there's something in the middle here that I can't see. We're at an impasse. And sometimes, when you come back later, the impasse isn't there. It's as confusing to me as it is to anyone.

Shprintzen:
What Works

Dr. Shprintzen

Generally, kids with VCFS need to be pushed. Most of the success stories we hear from people, they say the same thing: "Our parents really made us work." People with VCFS learn best by repetition, constant repetition. Now, this is not the way education is going these days. People are taught either by example or by concept. And concept involves executive functioning, and it involves problem solving, and that's the worst approach for kids with VCFS. What you need to do is teach them by using small concrete segments of information, and people with VCFS will learn that just fine.

Quinn is right: The short-term memory can be impaired. What happens sometimes is they'll learn it and it'll be gone tomorrow and then come back the next day. There's no predicting it. It's not that total memory or brain capacity is necessarily all that dramatically impaired; it's the way they retrieve information and the way they solve problems, and you have no way of knowing what stimulus it is that prompts them to recall that information. It's a matter of how the brain makes those connections, which can be quite hard to understand.

So I think you have to teach them differently. When your kids are teenagers, if you're sending them out with friends or someplace where money is going to be involved, give them a calculator. At school, see if the school will allow them to have a Palm Pilot or a BlackBerry where they can write down their assignments and even have alarms that tell them when they have to be in a certain place. You have to make an accommodation for where you know the weakness is, and then take a strength that they have, which is working with computers, and build on it.

People with VCFS are often great with computers—in part because computers are a lot like people with VCFS. Computers are very concrete. You can't skip steps. It follows a linear progression. In order to get from A to D, you still have to do B and C. Most people who are strong at problem solving and have good executive functioning go right from A to D. They skip the unnecessary parts of the process. People with VCFS can't do that.

As an example, take directions. I had a patient whose father wrote out a long list of directions for her to get to her grandmother's apartment. He told her that, to return, she should just do the reverse. She got there just fine, but she couldn't reverse them when it was time to go home, and she got lost. If he'd taken an extra few minutes to write the return directions out, instead of having her solve the problem in her head, she would have been fine. It might seem stupid or like a waste of time to somebody, but she would have made it back. Minor accommodation, positive out-

come. *That's how it should be for most people with VCFS. You find out how to take what you know about how they function and then work it into your plans for the day.*

Quinn may identify himself as dyslexic, but people with VCFS aren't dyslexic. Some of them are actually hyperlexic, meaning that they have very early letter and word recognition. The problem lies in decoding what they read. That's the problem. Not every doctor gives perfect advice or makes a perfect diagnosis, but dyslexia is not a feature of VCFS.

But a lot of people with VCFS have trouble absorbing information when they read it. One of the accommodations that we always recommend for kids with VCFS in school is for somebody to read questions to the kids, so that it's presented in a multi-sensory way, so that they hear it and see it. Also, we always recommend letting kids with VCFS take tests untimed, because they don't know how to manage time. We'll say, "Read the questions." And, in fact, we'll often ask, "Read the question to the child and then ask them if they understand the question, have them explain it back to you." This helps to bypass the executive functioning difficulties.

This also applies outside of the classroom. When kids with VCFS are young, we don't typically suggest that parents get them too significantly engaged in team sports. Again, some have done it successfully. But the process of learning the rules can be hard. Let's say soccer. Try to explain "offsides" to the average person, much less somebody who is not very good at problem solving—because that's where the big deficit is in cognition. While playing, being able to observe the playing field and pay attention to the other ten players on your team takes considerable problem-solving skills. People with VCFS are very concrete thinkers. Problem solving, a major component of executive functioning, is their biggest problem. Every study that has been done has shown that to be true.

So having ten other kids around you, and then not performing to the standards of the other ten kids, can be pretty cruel. And to keep screwing up on the field, and then still at the end of the day not being able to get the rules and understand how to play your position and that kind of thing, is very, very tough. Our suggestion is, get them involved with tennis, get them involved with horseback riding, judo and karate, things where your measure of success is not somebody else, but where your measure of success is you. You can always do better the next time.

This was all something that I learned from a parent, who said that their kid was a miserable failure playing basketball and soccer but started them in karate and they were great. Because how do you advance? You advance by being better than you were yesterday. You're not compared to the next kid. Classroom environments, team environments— they can be hard for kids with VCFS as they're growing up. Individual sports can be a great safe haven.

Surfing and Snowboarding

It was at about this time, when I was in high school, that I really started surfing and snowboarding. I'm not exaggerating when I say that those are the most important things I've ever done. Whenever I'm feeling down or having problems, I just jump in the water and everything's fine. When I was at Gow, I'd head off to snowboard whenever I could. At school, I was always struggling. I never did that well. But whenever I went out on a board, everything went back to normal.

I learned how to snowboard before I learned how to surf, because I was at Gow, where it was freezing all the time and we were about a million miles from the nearest ocean. Surfers were the ones who started snowboarding because they wanted to be able to surf down the mountain, and skateboarding had a major influence, too.

I had to work hard at learning to snowboard. I came back with bruises on my butt every day. But it was worth it. The first time I boarded down where there are no trails, the minute I got that taste of fresh powder, it was like a drug. You have to keep on doing it. You just want more of it.

The main reason I started surfing was that I saw some footage of Laird Hamilton, who is the best big-wave surfer in the world. He's my hero. I've watched every film and video about him that's out there. Watching him come down a sixty-foot wave, something that powerful, showed me what was possible. I think my parents got pretty sick of hearing about Laird, because he was all I talked about for a couple of years.

And now I'm talking about him just as much again, so I guess they're going to have to get used to it. At a party my parents had in April 2008, I met the great musician Ben Harper because his wife, Laura Dern, was at the party, too. I had seen Ben in some surf videos with Laird, so I asked if he knew him. He said he did, but he didn't make a big deal out of it.

Then, in July, this enormous surprise package comes in the mail for me, so big I couldn't even open it in the house. It was a long stand-up paddle board, maybe twenty feet long, about twice as big as any of my other surfboards. Now it fills up the whole front hall in our house. Laird made the board, and he signed it, "To Quinn, Mahalo and Aloha. Go Big. Laird." Ben had asked him to send it to me. When I got it, I felt as humble as I've ever felt in my life. I cried, I was so happy. It is the greatest gift I have ever received.

In East Hampton, with my long-board, and cousins Will and Lucy.

The funny thing is that I had dreamed about Laird the night before, a dream where he walked up to me, patted me on the head, and kept going. I woke up wondering what it meant, and then the board arrived.

*   *   *

From the start, even though I wasn't great at it, surfing just made me feel good. It's something that I worked hard at in order to be good at it. It takes so much concentration, and it's so much harder than it looks. It's rare that I ever really want to work hard at something, because I'm so afraid that I'll fail. Because of my difficulties, sometimes I feel that people expect me not to be able to do things, and that sometimes makes it harder to want to try.

But the minute you experience that feeling of riding that wave, it's the closest feeling to flying that you can get. And you're doing it without any help. You feel free. You're moving on something that you're not supposed to be on. I live for that feeling. We all came from the ocean. Everything came from the ocean. (And people think surfing started in Hawaii, but it actually came from the ancient Polynesians.)

Greg Noll, a professional surfer, says that the minute you catch the taste of coming down a wave, especially a big wave, it's very difficult not to want more. It's very, very addictive. Be careful, because you *will* get hooked. And I was hooked, right away.

I wasn't raised with any real form of religion, though I've always felt kind of spiritual. My parents just let me figure things like that out for myself. And when I go into the ocean, with a surfboard, that feels right. There's a movie called *In God's Hands,* about surfers, and they say that big waves are the greatest natural wonder of all the natural

wonders in the world. To ride waves is to put yourself in God's hands. In a way, it's almost like mountain climbing. You feel that you are conquering
something huge.

There's a famous photograph of Mavericks, a surf
break out near San Francisco, called "The Cathe-
dral." When I look at it, I do almost feel close to God
in a sense. God is huge. When you see a sixty-foot
wave, if you think we're the only thing, that we're
the most powerful thing in the world, then you have
some serious analyzing to do, as Laird once said.

When we go to Long Island in the summer, I
get up at 7:30 in the morning to hit the surf. Sometimes you have to wear a wetsuit, because the water
is freezing. My friends tend to tease me because I
don't normally like to get up early, but when I'm
near the ocean there's something in the air that
gets me going. I think it's because I hear the waves,
and there's something calling me, "Come, come." I
go to sleep listening to that sound.

The biggest attraction is the independence that
I feel when I'm surfing. Nobody is helping me.
When I catch the wave, it's just me and the ocean.
And if I catch it, in that moment I'm not thinking
about school, or VCFS, or anything like that. I'm just
thinking about catching the wave. And about how it
feels to have gotten on top of something so much
bigger and more powerful than myself. I think that's
what surfers are talking about when they say it's the
best feeling. (Some say it's more satisfying than sex.)

It's definitely the best feeling of accomplishment I've ever received from doing anything. It shows me what's possible. I'm not a pro surfer or anything close to it, but that's not the point. The best surfer is the one that's having the most fun. I've always had to struggle to get to where I want. When I'm in the water, everything feels normal. I feel normal. All my bodily aches and pains go away, and my head is clear. That doesn't happen many other places. It means more to me than anything else.

Transition
to College

When I graduated from Gow at twenty-one, I was older than most of the other kids graduating. (Briefly, being older made me somewhat popular, because I could buy beer.) I had left the Lab School a little older than your regular freshman, and Gow held me back for a year right when I arrived to allow me to catch up to the other kids.

As I said before, there are about five generations of my family that went to Harvard. My dad went to Harvard, and my grandfather, my great-grandfather, my great-great-grandfather, and so on. I did and didn't feel pressured to go to Harvard. But it wasn't an option.

I wish I could have gone to Harvard. My parents didn't care that it was out of the question. I mean, they'd have loved it if I could have gotten into an Ivy League school, but they just wanted a college where I felt comfortable.

I think parents who put pressure on their kids to get into great schools or else, that really screws the kids up. It just makes them uncomfortable, and they're not going to do well in high school because they have all this pressure on them. And it makes them worried: What if I don't get into that school? Harvard or Yale or Princeton or whatever. Will my parents still love me? I think getting into any school is good. Some kids don't go to college at all.

The college question was hard for me, because while I was still at school, some of my friends were going to the most prestigious universities. My oldest friend, Teddy Jones, got into Harvard, and my friend Lacie went to Trinity College. My friend from the Lab School, Peter Lockett, who is a math and science genius, went to Brown. Now he's an aerospace engineer out in California. He had a lot of trouble reading, but he made it through Brown with a tutor. (He jokes that he never even opened a book.)

I'm a big believer that history repeats itself. And I think that we are our fathers. Boys are their fathers. I've heard that all Bradlees were late bloomers. I may not have had the chance to go to Harvard, at least not yet, but that doesn't mean that great things aren't still ahead for me.

In general, I think the pressure of our family name and history is harder for my older brother, who's Ben Bradlee *Junior*. I have both of my parents' names put together. I'm Josiah Quinn Crowninshield Bradlee, and there's only one of me.

Despite the high expectations, I like being part of my dad. There's a picture of my dad in his senior year in high school, when he was graduating, and there's a picture of me at the same age, taken decades later. If you put them together, they look a lot alike. Many of the Bradlee men look like each other at a particular moment in their lives. But it doesn't stay that way. When you have VCFS, sometimes your eyebrows are a bit more prominent. When I looked at my dad's picture, I saw that he had the thickest eyebrows in the world when he was my age. It makes me feel better. And it's another one of those areas where I have the same old question: Am I like this because I have VCFS, or because that's just how my family is anyway?

The other thing my mom says I've inherited from my dad is the old Bradlee charm. It comes in handy sometimes. It works much better for me with adults than it does with other kids. But I'll take something over nothing any day.

When it came time for me to go to college, according to my mom, the ole Bradlee charm came in handy. Everybody recommended that I go to Landmark College, which is a great college for kids with learning disabilities, up in a little town in Vermont called Putney. (I had already been to Landmark summer school for high school kids a few times, which is in Beverly, Massachusetts, where my dad grew up.) When we went up to Vermont for a visit, we met with the president or one of the higher-ups for a while. I don't know whether I was already going to get in or not, but I do know that when I walked out of the meeting, my parents both agreed that I'd had the ole charm going. I got in.

Animal
House

First things first, there were girls at Landmark. Finally! It was kind of a shocker, coming from an all-guys prep school. The ratio was about three boys to every one girl, but still. They were there.

Part of my nervousness around girls was that I had very, very limited experience talking to girls my age. I had some friends in D.C., like Lacie and Jackie (a good friend from the Lab School), but Lacie and I were basically born together and we're almost like cousins or siblings or something. This was my first real experience socializing with girls.

One of the big factors kids with VCFS struggle with is that we have a hard time reading social cues. It's different from a strict learning disability, or maybe not. Who knows? But when I first got to college, I had no idea when I was talking to a girl whether she wanted to talk to me or not. (Truth be told, I still don't.)

My friends who had better luck with the ladies would tell me when a girl was into me, but it was never clear to me. I couldn't get to the point when I could tell whether a girl liked me, or whether she liked me in a way that would lead to us having sex. (I'd be lying if I said that wasn't one of the most important aspects. By the time I was twenty-one, I was pretty psyched to get laid.) It didn't help any that the Dexedrine I was taking for my ADD was drying out my lips so bad that I had to walk around with Chap-Stick and water all the time. Hard to be a chick magnet like that.

The social scene at Landmark was obviously really different from Gow. Girls have a way of changing the mood. The campus was a dry campus, but there were lots of off-campus parties. This was my first real experience with parties where there was a lot of alcohol and drugs, and my first experience with drinking. (My parents would let me have wine with dinner, but that doesn't really count.)

I'm well aware of the alcoholism that's in my family, on both sides. Both of my grandfathers were big drinkers. I think my parents think about it, too. Dandy used to say that it was his Irish heritage that caused him to drink—the whole "Quinn" thing. It's always in the back of my head if I'm going to go out drinking or whatever, that I need to try to stay in control of myself.

I do like the sensation. It's a good sensation. But the threat of throwing up keeps me from going too far. I hate being sick more than anything, maybe because I was sick so much as a kid. But I do love getting a little buzz.

At Landmark, there were a number of really nice kids, kids who seemed really cool, who were drinking all the time. After a while, at those kinds of parties, it basically just looks like a battlefield. Everybody's on the floor, drunk and stupid. What's the fun in that?

Being in Vermont, there wasn't a whole lot else to do. A lot of people smoked pot. I did, too, every once in a while, but that was about as far as I would go. I never really got stupid off of it, where you just laugh all the time. But I didn't really do as much of it as some of the other kids did.

I think kids who have learning disabilities might get even more of a thrill out of drinking and smoking than most people. Because I think they probably feel down a little bit more than everybody else, so it just cheers them up. Also, it's something that "normal" kids do a lot of, and so I think sometimes by partying, LD kids feel like it helps them fit in. Sometimes if you're drinking with friends, it's kind of hard not to, because you don't want to be the one that's chicken. I just don't like getting sick.

Socially, the best part of Landmark was that I lived with my friend Sean Frost almost the whole time. We met at Landmark summer school while I was at Gow. We didn't really like the people we were rooming with that summer, so we decided to room together. When I got to Landmark College, I had no idea Sean was there. I was walking on the campus one day and I heard somebody say my name. There was Sean, standing right there. We ended up moving in with each other again.

We got along really well. We knew each other's inner secrets and everything, and we still stay in touch. He just moved to L.A. with our other friend, Scott. Those two guys were my closest friends at Landmark. Scott's the kind of kid who can make you piss your pants, no matter what mood you're in. I miss them both today.

Film

      Academically, I didn't do that well at Landmark. I'm not proud of it, but the truth is that I didn't try as hard as I could have. Ever since I was a little kid, I've had a problem with motivation. I know a lot of people who are like me in this regard. Everybody would like to go to the gym more and lose ten pounds or something. But it's worse than that for me. It's been one of my biggest problems in life.

      I was so sick when I was a little kid that I got used to having people do things for me all the time. As I've gotten older, I've had to get used to doing those things for myself. But if you ask my mom, she'll tell you I can still be pretty good at getting people to do things for me.

      It's just hard for me to find motivation sometimes. It was true at Landmark, and it's been true since then. When I hear someone say that whether or not I do anything or succeed or fail that I'll still have a nice life, it makes me feel like a rich prick.

The truth is, by some definition, I am. But I know that about myself.

And I still have more problems than most people in terms of the way my brain works. I'm proof that money doesn't solve everything. It helps. I had tutors and I got to travel to cool places with my family and all of that. But none of those things could make my disability go away. I'd trade off all the wealth for a brain that worked right.

Could I still have worked harder at Landmark? I would have said no if you'd asked me at the time, but I know now that the answer is yes. I probably should have had a tutor there, too—that might have helped.

The one bright area for me at Landmark was that I discovered film. They had a great professor, Christina Nova, who taught film and really knew her shit. I was stuck in this art class, where you sat there and drew all day, and being ADD, it was my worst nightmare. But then my adviser said that some-body had dropped out of the film class, and I could go if I wanted to.

Right away, I felt a crazy amount of fear. Film was something I had always wanted to explore. I spent a lot of time alone as a kid, so I'd seen a lot of movies and felt that I knew a lot about film already from that. And then you realize, well, what if I'm not good at it and it's the only thing that I really want to do? Then what? But I didn't really have time to think about it, because I got into the class two weeks after it started. I was able to catch up, and from then on I really felt that film was what I was going to do.

One of the things that inspired me about film was surfing. The first time I saw a documentary on the big wave surfers, guys coming down forty-five-foot waves, I thought, "That's the most amazing thing I've ever seen in my life." I wanted to try to find things like that that I could show to people. That something so much bigger than yourself can be conquered shows you what's possible, what can be done.

I loved the film class right from the start. With the learning disabilities that I've had, I've always been a little more visual. And being in film class at Landmark just felt right. I did extra work. I went to the editing room when school was over, and after what felt like a minute or two it would be 8:00 at night. It was like meditation. When I got done with the yearlong class, my teacher said that I was one of the best documentarians she'd ever seen. She thought I had real potential. And I believed her. And for me, that's rare.

The other really good experience I had at Landmark was with a psychology professor, Rebecca Matte. She was one of the best teachers I ever had. Once she gave an assignment, and I did it completely wrong, different from everybody else. But she claimed that I had done it in such an amazingly wrong way that she thought it was extraordinary, and she kept it to show to everybody. If you did something wrong, she wasn't going to embarrass you.

We all got one-on-one time with Rebecca Matte if we needed help, and she would specifically take time off to work with me. When she could have been sitting at home with her family, she was helping me. And I really, really appreciated that. She helped me figure out that my absolute maximum attention span is four hours. I think it is safe to say that we both learned that the hard way.

No Cure

Although by the time I was out of Landmark my physical VCFS difficulties were less severe than they were when I was a kid, they didn't go away—not completely. They never will. It's something you live with when you have VCFS.

This is a small example, but take Landmark. Once while I was there, I broke out into hives so badly that I had to be sent home. There were a couple of other kids with hives at the time, but I got them worse than anybody. That's what always seems to happen, because of my weak immune system.

I think in that particular case my reaction was a combination of trying to keep up with all of my schoolwork, which I didn't do a very good job of, and finding out that a friend of mine from Landmark summer school had to go to rehab. When I got home, I had so many hives that I couldn't walk for three days. Little red bumps sprung up all over me, from my head to my ugly toes, all because of stress.

Much worse than the little stuff were the migraines that continued to hound me. I started to get them when I was about fifteen, and I got them all through Gow and Landmark and even a little beyond. (I haven't had a really bad one in a long time, but I'm keeping my fingers crossed.) They're almost like seizures. Sometimes I lose consciousness. They'll start with a sharp pain in the right side of my head, and then I'll get very weak all of a sudden, and then I start vomiting. Not fun.

One of the doctors who saw me during a bad migraine when I was seventeen described it like this:

> In July, on Long Island, he was playing tennis and golf, and had a coke. He developed a severe headache and vomited. He was seen in the Emergency Room because he could not drink and was very weak. His eyes rolled back, his face was pale, and his lips were blue. After this episode, his mother spoke with some experts in the field of the syndrome [VCFS] who stated that these children develop episodes of transient calcium disorders and needed to drink plenty of water. . . . The week prior to his consultation he again was in the Carribean [*sic*] snorkeling in the morning. He developed a headache, took some Advil, vomited, and began to go into what his mother described as a shock-like state. He was treated with intravenous fluids overnight.

You can imagine how much fun it is for me and for
my parents when stuff like that happens. We've figured out that it has something to do with hydration
and the sun, but I never really know when it's going
to happen. One time, I was out on my friend's boat
in the sun all day and drank beer without any
water . . . that time I guess I was kind of asking for it.

Most people who suffer from migraines can
carry around strong beta-blockers that might be
able to give them some relief. But because of my
heart, I can't take beta-blockers. As a secondary effect of VCFS, I have something called Wenckebach
syndrome, which is a kind of blockage in the arteries
in my heart, and if you have any kind of congestive
heart failure, you can't take beta-blockers because
they can make it worse (for a series of complicated
medical reasons).

If I go to a hospital, whoever is treating me needs
to be aware of what I can and can't take. Sometimes
people think my mom goes a little overboard, that
she's overprotective. But when she goes crazy about
this particular thing, she's right. If some intern
or something gave me beta-blockers, it could—not
necessarily would—screw with my heart and maybe
even kill me. So she rides pretty hard on that one.

As I've gotten older, it seems like some of the
worst physical stuff from VCFS has tailed off a little
bit, though I still get migraines on occasion. But long
term, there's stuff I'll never be able to do because of
VCFS. I have scoliosis, so it hurts to sit or stand for

long periods of time unless I'm in a comfortable chair. Because of my heart surgery, my chest is a little bit underdeveloped, so if I want to get the ladies at the beach I have to work on my pecs some. After Landmark, I had to have surgery on one foot and then on the other, because the bones were malformed. It took two months to recover from the surgery on each foot.

My heart condition also means I can't follow my father and grandfather and serve our country in the armed forces. I still have tinnitus, and sometimes I just feel really crappy for no reason. My sinuses are pretty bad, too, even though I just had surgery to try to drain them. I do this little snort to clear them, which isn't that attractive and can be embarrassing around girls. I grind my teeth at night, which is sometimes part of the ringing I get in my ears. (Some people in college said my teeth grinding sounded like crickets, and others said it sounded like a bomb factory.) I'm also so prone to infection that I can't even have acupuncture for fear that any one of the needles, if not cleaned properly, could cause an infection that could hurt me. I used to have to go on antibiotics if I had dental work or any other invasive procedure, though apparently that's not always necessary any more.

If you have VCFS, there are a lot of things going on with your body, all the time. It's not just LD problems in the classroom. This is the stuff I have; if you're somebody else, like Dr. Shprintzen says with the "variable expression," you'll have something else. But it'll be something. It's really just a question of how you deal with it. I try not to get down about it, but sometimes it's hard not to.

Learning
Outside of School

I had two pretty big experiences outside of Landmark, during the summers, that really made their mark on me. The first one was an archaeological dig at two sites in historic St. Mary's City, in southern Maryland. The second was a trip to Alaska with the National Outdoor Leadership School, NOLS.

On the archaeological dig, I was with "regular" kids. Aside from a summer camp I went to, it was one of my first mainstream experiences. The good part was that it wasn't in a classroom. I worked mostly at the St. John's site, where we were excavating an old printing house from the late seventeenth century. They didn't train us all that much. They tell you a little bit, but they took us down to Jamestown to see how it was done there.

In archaeology, your biggest tool is your eyes. I'm such a visual learner that I took to it right away. (To really do well, obviously there's more training involved, and dirt-matching labels and all that, but you could get up to entry-level speed pretty fast.)

We worked from 8:00 in the morning until 4:30 or so in the afternoon, when it would usually rain. Now that I look back, I wish I'd stayed at the dormitory more. I had a room there, but I stayed across the river at Porto Bello. Which was probably a mistake, because I could have hung out with the other kids more. And that's what I think my parents wanted. If I'd known better, I probably would have done it. It would have helped me socialize and make friends. They were really nice kids. But when you have a house across the river, it's kind of hard not to want to stay there.

When we were at the foundation site, we were mainly looking for pipe stems. If you found a bowl, you were really, really lucky, because that's the first thing to break and disintegrate. We were also looking for rare seventeenth-century glass beads, and for coins.

One day, as I was digging, my trowel scraped something. It sounded like a penny. And my heart just started pounding, I was so excited. We're not supposed to take things out, we're supposed to dig around them. But I couldn't help myself, and I reached in and took it out. It was a Lord Calvert coin, from 1647. I was the first one to find a coin that year. Of course, the day after somebody else found a coin, but still. I gave it to the professor.

I remember reading an article about how marine archaeologists found a sunken ship off the coast of Greece, 3,000 years old, and the ship was still intact. They found wine jugs, unopened. That's the thing with history, and why I loved archaeology so much. You're literally digging up history. It's not in a book. You're there, feeling it, smelling it, seeing it. It's learning in a different way. It was a better way for me, I think.

And also, working on the dig gave me some skills for digging around at Porto Bello. I haven't found anything all that much, but now I know a little better what I'm doing. A little bit can make all the difference.

The NOLS trip was probably a bigger deal for me in terms of learning about myself. It was a monthlong kayaking trip in Alaska. There would be zero communication with my parents, which was a first for me. My dad didn't even want me to go. He didn't think I could hack it. And I barely did.

Where we were kayaking was absolutely beautiful, but when we first got there, I was miserable. Really miserable. It was summer, but it was in Alaska. I think the coldest it got was 48 degrees, and it was pouring down rain most of the time. By the third day, all of our gear was soaking wet. We would paddle all day on the ocean, and then we camped on the beaches of the islands. I think our shortest paddle was maybe eight miles or so.

It was really hard. I wanted to go home. I had no idea what I was getting into, and I figured my dad was right. And so I asked the instructors what would

Looking out at an unbeatable view in Alaska.

happen if I wanted to go home, and I asked if they had ever evacuated somebody out.

They said they had, but it was only because of a serious injury. If I wanted to go, all of us would have to turn around—we were already about fifty miles out—and end the trip short.

This was one of the biggest moments in my life. I really wanted to go home. I had to think hard about who I was. They would have taken me back if I'd said they had to, but I realized I'd never forgive myself for doing that. I decided I couldn't live with myself if that happened. So I just said, "Screw it." I stayed.

The rest of the trip was difficult. I don't think it was only me who was thinking, "What the hell am I doing out here?" I also learned that I have some real problems with organization. .

I struggled every day, because I would pack the same stuff in the same bags, and then I would forget which one I'd put my clothes in. It was sometimes impossible for me to find anything—even though I'd packed my own bags. It drove me crazy. Sometimes our stuff wouldn't always be in our kayak, it'd be in somebody else's kayak, and I'd always be the last person to find what I was looking for.

At one point, all the kids went out on their own to spend a night alone in the wilderness. The instructors held me back with them. I don't know exactly why they didn't want me to go. I was a little depressed about it, because I felt outed.

But then one day we were about 150 miles out or so, and we maybe had one more long day of paddling before we reached the end of the trip. We took a floating break, which is where you just sit there and float. And all of a sudden, this giant tail, about a twenty-foot span, comes out of the water. Right next to me and my friend Laura. It was a humpback whale. We were so stunned. They didn't really warn us about whales. And we were all so floored by the beauty of this creature, this hump coming out of the water, and the tail. We saw whales often for the rest of the trip, and I never would have seen them if I had gone home.

It was hard, but I did it. I learned that people, if they absolutely have to, will push themselves. It was in me to get through it. I think it shocked a lot of people, including my parents, that I was actually able to do it. Like math class, sometimes things that look hard aren't that hard if you do them. Or even if they are hard, they end up being worth it. Humans are adaptable creatures.

*   *   *

It's often really hard to know what's "normal" for every kid and what's happening only to me because of VCFS. It took me a while to figure out that some of the trouble I had in social situations had a lot to do with VCFS, that it's "normal" for kids with VCFS to have that kind of problem. It was one of the ways that being diagnosed was sort of a relief. Dr. Shprintzen can tell you the reasons for this a lot better than I can.

More from Dr. Shprintzen

The things that can be fixed physically, that's not as much of a problem. The success rate with those procedures is very high.

But social maturity is a big issue. Where we find there are significant issues for kids with VCFS is with their ability to read social cues. One of the experiments that is being done here at Upstate now, in the lab of Dr. Wendy Kates, an eminent researcher in VCFS, and in Upstate's VCFS International Center, is an experiment looking at recognizing emotional responses in faces. We're doing this as part of a functional MR (Magnetic Resonance) study. So that you're

*in the MR scanner, and you're presented with a series of
faces, and you're asked to match the emotion to the face. So
we'll show somebody who's surprised, somebody who's frightened, somebody who's laughing. And using the functioning
MR, we take a look to see which parts of the brain are becoming active, and we compare that to a series of control
subjects.*

*We find completely different patterns for the people
with VCFS. We also find that they're not particularly good
at recognizing the difference between frightened and happy,
or surprised and frightened. So their ability to read social
cues is different.*

*Some of that is experience. Often, kids with VCFS
aren't integrated completely into the full world of social
exposure, especially chronologically. Their chronological
years are often in advance of their social maturity. They
tend to have fewer friends than other people. That's one
place where Quinn really excels. He's got lots of friends
now, people who are there for him.*

*But when they're not getting it socially—let me put it
this way. If you were talking to somebody and they weren't
getting you, but you didn't know they had VCFS, you
would just say, "Eh, they're just dense." They're just sort of
not getting it. But with VCFS, this is something that is
biological. It's built into the way they function. And so
that makes it more difficult for them to integrate, to find the
right place for themselves. And that's no different for Quinn.*

*If you take the normal curve, relative to cognitive per-
formance in a broad sense, people with VCFS are skewed
just slightly to the left. So that their average IQ is lower than*

it is in the general population; their average social skill scores are lower than they are in the general population; their developmental milestones are a little bit behind. They're not grossly behind, they're not grossly impaired—at least, not the vast majority. But they're just shifted. In IQ, it's a little more than twenty points.

That doesn't mean that there aren't some who have average or above average IQs. There are. But it's the whole package of temperament, maturity, social cues, and the rest of it. There are consistencies in the pattern that we see that are more predictable than you would have in the general population, because we have a biological cause behind this. So we try, in our efforts to counsel parents appropriately, to let them devise strategies.

Where the issue is learning and education, kids with VCFS do progress, but over time they tend to compare less well with their peers than they did early on. Usually in kindergarten, first grade, when learning is relatively simple and not a lot of executive functioning (or frontal lobe) stuff is going on, the kids aren't at much of a disadvantage. It's usually when they reach junior high school and high school where they really start to separate from their peers in terms of academic performance.

And that's because as you get older, the curriculum starts to get loaded with things like trigonometry and literature and interpretation and so on. That's a particularly difficult spot for them, so they tend to look worse academically over time. Some of them hold their own, sort of tread water, but they don't typically get good grades.

But usually I like to speak to them more about this: What's the purpose of the education here? What is it that you're after? If a VCFS patient struggles in a normal curriculum, you really should be thinking about how you want to modify that and make accommodations, whether it's in a vocational path or a more practical academic path.

But most high schools are graduating kids to go to college. They don't see their role as being a terminal point in education, as it used to be in the 1940s, the 1950s. Now, even college is sometimes not a terminal point. Lots of people are getting master's degrees or doctorates.

So what I usually advise parents to see is to try to grasp where they see their exit strategy being. What's the purpose of the education? A child with VCFS is probably not going to be an accountant, and almost certainly not a nuclear physicist. This is not a mark of shame or failure. Those simply aren't the skills they have. So you can't aim an education toward those things. Where is it that you want to aim the education? What is it that you want the kid to be doing? You can look at people with VCFS as being limited and having fewer choices, or you can simply look at it from the perspective of life in general. Which is, everybody has limitations.

After Landmark

I never graduated from college. The experience at Landmark was harder for me than I thought it would be. I was really struggling with studying, and I felt like I couldn't stay afloat, and I didn't want to, either. I don't blame that on Landmark. It's just how it was. My mom offered to get me a private tutor if I'd go back, but I just didn't want to go back.

The thing was, I discovered that film was something I was really excited about and passionate for. So when I came home from Landmark after two years, I decided to try taking some classes at American University. It was closer to home, too—basically at home. I wanted to try the challenge of going to a "regular" school for once. I thought maybe that would inspire me to work harder.

AU was a shocker. At Gow, my biggest class was about six people or so, and at Landmark it was about fifteen. At AU, in order to take a film class I had to take a journalism class with 100 kids, and also a photography class.

AU made Landmark look like kindergarten. I passed the two classes I took, but only barely. AU was so much harder, it was almost impossible for me. Even with a tutor who came to class with me, I was barely hacking it—and I was only taking two courses.

When you're ADD, it's hard to sit in a chair for three hours at once. I had trouble understanding the lectures whenever I thought they weren't interesting. I don't focus well when I think something's uninteresting. I've heard this is true of my dad, too. Hard to know what's normal and what's me. But if I hadn't had the tutor, I wouldn't have made it. He kept track of my schedule, and what was due when.

The environment at AU was so different from Landmark, Gow, every other place I'd been. Everywhere else, I had people getting me where I needed to be and telling me what I needed to be doing. Not at AU. It was hard for me.

On top of that, because it was a "regular" school, the way I had to take tests made me stand out. I didn't take extra time for the tests, like I could at Gow or Landmark, because I hated to be the last one to leave. But I also hated taking the tests orally. I felt pressured to hurry with my answers. At Gow and Landmark, tests were timed, but you had so much time that they were basically untimed, and everybody was on the same page. You never felt different for doing it your own way.

I always felt a little embarrassed when I took tests, because I'm afraid of them, and I'm afraid of the pressure. I think tests are a bad way to see what someone knows. The one test I almost enjoyed was a take-home test that I took to a café and worked on. I felt free and confident. It was the only test I passed at AU without help. If I feel someone is watching over me, I'm not going to do well. My advice to other LD kids who are facing tests in normal school is not to be afraid to ask for more time, or to ask for a different room.

One class I took at AU was photography. I liked taking pictures but didn't really enjoy the work in the darkroom so much. Probably not the best fit for me. The other class was journalism. I never raised my hand. I was intimidated. One of the reasons I was nervous is because of who my parents are. Once I say Ben Bradlee and Sally Quinn are

A recent shot of me with my parents.

my parents, I always feel like the expectations for me just grow and grow, and it makes it harder for me to succeed.

Journalism is in my blood, I guess, but I'm not drawn to it the way my parents are. Because of my disability, but also because I've had such bad experiences in the past. Pretty soon after starting the journalism class, I was kind of like, "Why put that kind of pressure on yourself?" I'm never going to know a Deep Throat, or meet a Deep Throat.

(For those of you who don't know, "Deep Throat" was Bob Woodward's secret source during Watergate. They would meet in a parking lot. Turns out he was the number two guy at the FBI, but nobody knew it was him except for Woodward and Bernstein and my dad. The information he gave Woodward helped them make stories in the *Washington Post* that eventually led Nixon to resign. Deep Throat is named after a porno film that came out at the same time. I didn't realize this until I typed the words into the computer at the library when I was at Gow and about a million porn sites came up.)

At AU, even though it was hard for me, I had to stick it out. We had to make a documentary at the end of my journalism class, and Tom Brokaw let me take a group to interview him. It was really nice of him to do it. When we were making the groups, everybody in class wanted to be in my group. For one day, I was the most popular kid, but then after the documentary I went back to being a nobody.

In general, I didn't make many friends at AU. It was hard because I was living at home, and at AU I pretty much just went to class and didn't hang out much afterward. The one good thing for me at AU was that I met a girl, Mary. The best part of it was that she noticed me, instead of vice versa. It made me feel like things were changing, that I was getting better, that I was doing something right.

One day in class, the teacher asked, "Who wants to partner with Quinn?" And Mary raised her hand. I had talked to her before. The first time I saw her I introduced myself to her, and whatever I said obviously made some impression.

I'll never forget that day, because that doesn't happen to me much. It's rare for a girl to notice me and want to work with me.

When we went up to see Brokaw for the interview, we shared a hotel room and talked all night. I never made any moves. I don't really know if I could have or not. I probably should have, but I wasn't sure it was right for me to, and I didn't want to make her feel uncomfortable. We're not in touch anymore, but I was happy to have known her.

Film
School

After AU, I figured that my schooling days were over. I couldn't keep up there, and I didn't want to keep up there. It was a whole different league. It was not my league. I'm cool with that.

So the question was, what next? Going to a mainstream college and graduating and heading off to a "regular" job wasn't in the deck of cards for me.

I had to figure out what I really wanted to do and what I could do. And the only thing I'd ever loved (at least that I could make any money off of) was film. If they would pay me to surf every day that would be sweet, but I doubt it. Film was the only thing that ever stood out to me as something that I really wanted to do.

Both of my parents thought that film made sense for me at that stage, as something that I should focus on. My dad thought it was a good idea, but as he always does, he wondered if I'd stick to it. My mom thought it made sense because I liked it, and I was

good at it. Having them both behind me, believing
that I could do it if I set my mind to it, was really
important.

If I wanted to have a career making documentaries or anything else, there were still things I knew
I needed to learn. As a result, I interned with a filmmaker in D.C. named Mark Muheim. He is a great
guy. We had the idea of doing something about
VCFS at some point, but after a little while interning,
I figured out that I probably needed more training.

One of our good family friends had sent his
son to the New York Film Academy and recommended it. My mom called the school and told
them a little bit about me, and they were willing to
take me. I knew this would be different from AU,
because it was pretty strictly focused on what I
wanted to learn.

There are a bunch of different programs at
the NYFA. There's a yearlong program, but there are
also weeklong and monthlong programs where you
learn different skills. I was planning to do the yearlong program, but we decided it'd be better if I just
tried some of the monthlong programs to see how
it went.

Some of the classes at the NYFA were extremely
intense. We had orientation for about an hour before they basically threw us to the wolves. Some of
the classes were five hours long. I took mostly direct-
ing courses, though there was one mandatory acting
course. (To be a director, you have to know how an

actor thinks and feels.) And we took an editing class where we learned how to use Final Cut Pro.

My mom decided before I left that I would probably need some help getting through all of my classes. I'd had tutors other places, as I said earlier. My mom asked Michael Young, who ran the NYFA, if there was anybody he knew who might be willing to help me as a kind of tutor. He recommended this guy named Justin.

Justin Lee Peterson

Justin Lee Peterson was one of the nicest people I have ever met in my life. He was a filmmaker who had gone to New York University for three years and helped start a film school in Florence, Italy. I think he knew more about film than a lot of the professors at the NYFA. He wasn't just my tutor. He was like a guide, at the academy and in life. Most important, he became an unbelievable friend. He always understood what I needed.

He helped me in all the classes, and he helped me outside of class. He always included me in the films he was making. There were times where I didn't want to go, and he would drag my ass out because he knew I would benefit from the experience. He would give me a small part, either in the film or in the making of the film.

He made one film about the Italian mafia with his roommate, Fulvio Brembilla—also a great guy. It was a short film, basically just his roommate playing about twenty different guys. Justin gave me a little scene where mafia guys dragged me away after a major beatdown. He would always make sure that my name was in the credits somehow, that I had something to do with the film. I felt really close with him, because he always included me. Most people probably wouldn't, at least not right away. He did it right away.

All week we were in class, and then over the weekends we'd have assignments to make short films. I didn't love that, but at least we were outside. We all had to help each other out and make each other's films, whether we wanted to or not. That's just how it worked.

One weekend in the fall, I went out to Brooklyn to help a buddy from class make a three-minute film. I was living in a shithole at the time—my mom says that's "too glowing" a description—but this guy had it even worse than I did. There's always some-body who has it worse than you do.

It took us about six hours to make a three-minute film. No joke. It took almost two hours to get the lighting right. It was one of our first assign-ments, so we struggled a bit. It's not that it's that hard, or that we didn't know how to do it, because we'd been trained to do it. It's just getting it right—lighting, then setting up the camera and getting all the actors in positions—takes a while. Being on set and actually doing it is where you really learn. You can only learn so much in the classroom.

In the end, we did more editing than anything else. At film school, you actually do very little shoot-ing of films. Most of your time is spent at the com-puter, editing.

I probably learned more from Justin than from anybody else. He was $33,000 in debt, just from making movies, because that's what he loved to do. The reason he made films was because he was going to keep on doing it until he hit it big. And some-times you don't hit it big. But he was more willing to help me right away than any other teacher I've ever had.

Justin wanted to make his first feature film, and I was going to quit the NYFA to work with him . . . but somebody (you'll never guess) didn't agree with that idea. In the end, she was probably right. And even Justin, trying to be a teacher, said it was prob-ably better for me to stay, that everybody needs to go through film school.

We did go out to Aspen together to make a short documentary on snowboarding. I interviewed the head of the X Games, and a couple of the riders. ESPN let me use some footage. Naturally at the time, I had the dream that I would end up making sports documentaries for ESPN, but it didn't work out quite like that. It wasn't my greatest film anyhow.

Sometimes when you don't think you're benefiting from something, you end up benefiting a lot more than you realize. That's been true for me throughout my life. And one thing did stick with me from film school. The first thing they teach you is: Stick with what you know. It's good advice.

Living in New York was the first time I really lived on my own. It was a mixed bag. I got the apartment through the NYFA, and it was pretty nasty. It was cool that it was in SoHo, but mice had eaten holes in the doors and walls and the whole hallway stunk like trash. I'm kind of spoiled, but everybody who saw it (including Lisa) agreed that it was pretty bad. I didn't really mind, except for the rats when I took the trash out. At first, I was sort of like, "This sucks. I have to do everything." But then you realize it's kind of cool. You have all this freedom.

I had roommates through the school. There was an English girl, who was really nice, and there was a model, who was beautiful but strange. She taught me that just because you're the hottest girl in the world doesn't mean you're going to end up being the nicest girl in the world.

The best was Fernando von Christian, one of the nicest guys I ever met. He lived with me for the fall. A great, great guy, one of the best roommates I've ever had. His uncle was the number one Formula One driver in the world. He would take me out to the clubs with him, and we got along great. When he left, I ended up spending a lot more time on my own, which was tough.

The thing is, I loved New York. At first I never wanted to go back home, never wanted to leave. I thought I was going to stay in the city for the rest of my life. But by the third month, I was struggling a little bit. I became more independent after a week in New York than I had been for my entire adult life. But when I got done with a year at the NYFA, I was ready to come home.

A year after I got back, we heard the tragic news that Justin had been killed in an accident. At about 2:30 in the afternoon, he fell six stories from the ledge outside of his apartment. The story goes deeper than that, but I don't really like to talk about it. I don't think he was trying to kill himself or anything, but the whole thing is just awful. I saw his mother afterwards. Justin was her youngest kid, and I just thought, "This is what depression is." I could see and feel her pain.

In some ways, Justin was why I wanted to write this book. He helped me. He really, honestly, actually helped me. I think he had a lot to do with the other kids at the NYFA liking me. I think if I had been there without Justin, I wouldn't have been as popular as I was. He was a guy that everybody liked. He was a guy who, if you were in trouble, would be there, and he'd kick the other guy's ass in a minute, without hesitation. He'd take me out drinking and show me how to have fun, but he'd never let me do anything stupid.

That's the best kind of friend anybody can have. I never had a bad time with him, not once. Wherever you are now, Justin, my family and I will always remember you.

Isolation

Justin stands out to me so much because for a lot of my childhood, at least the parts that I remember, I felt invisible. Not because people didn't pay attention to me. It's not like I was criminally neglected or anything. But at times, I just felt like a ghost.

I think part of that's just being an only kid around adults a lot. When I'm around my little nieces and nephews, I see how adults don't always respond to them. They don't always pay attention to what kids say. Adults think that the kid will probably forget, or that what the kid said is not that important.

I was different as a little kid. For one thing, I had trouble talking. My left vocal cord was paralyzed at one point, and my voice was really scratchy and hard to understand. I can't tell you how many times I would be at dinner—with anybody, didn't matter who—and I would hear something about a subject I knew something about and start talking. I would be able to tell that people weren't really listening. It was like I didn't exist. There were a few times I was basically screaming, and people still kept interrupting me to have other conversations. Most times I would just say, "The hell with them," and go into the other room and put on the TV.

Sometimes it even happened in family settings. We took a trip to Turkey in 2001, right before September 11, to celebrate my dad's eightieth birthday. A lot of our friends were there. One night everybody was giving speeches about how great my dad was, and what a great kid I was, and blah blah blah and blah blah blah. But when I would try to say anything, people just kept interrupting me.

Later on in the trip, the entire group of people left for dinner without me. It was like *Home Alone*. Again, it's not because I was criminally neglected or anything. I was in my room by myself, with my earphones on, and everybody else was having drinks someplace else. But they didn't seem to know that I wasn't with them. And I was kind of depressed about that. It's hard not to be. I just sat there feeling all lonely and mad at myself, but then I got my act together, went to the concierge, and caught a cab. I ended up almost beating them there. (In my parents' defense, they say they both thought I'd gone in one of the other cars. They didn't realize what had happened until I walked in on my own.)

Feeling left out also happened at school, or on trips I would take with other kids over the summer.

When I would start talking, somebody else would start talking, and then everybody would focus on the other person. And I'd say, "Excuse me, but I was saying something."

Sometimes, when everybody is having a good time, I think people forget that I have a learning disability, that I process things differently. My disability is relatively mild. Sometimes people might think I understand everything, or am completely "typical," when I'm not. It's hard to deal with. But you've got to deal with it and make the best of it.

When people ignore you, it's hurtful. I don't care who you are. But you do learn from that experience how other people feel when you ignore them. I watch for that in myself a lot now, and I don't do it. I don't know if going through my situation has made me any more sensitive to other people, because my mom is really sensitive, too. But I'll take sensitive. Girls like sensitive guys.

The other thing that was hard to figure out about feeling ignored was how much was just normal social stuff and how much was due to having VCFS or speaking difficulties or being learning disabled. I really don't remember when I realized that I was any different from other kids. I grew up in learning-disabled schools and hospitals, so I just thought that that was how all kids were. Nothing seemed strange.

I do remember meeting Dr. Shprintzen for the first time. And he said VCFS wasn't the biggest deal. But you do start to realize that you really are different, that this is something that you're going to have to live with. I try as hard as I can not to let it get me down.

There are times where I feel so isolated. I get really upset about it, and then maybe I overreact. I get depressed. I'm not perfect. There are times when I feel so awful, physically and mentally, that it hurts to keep my eyes open for a long time. I feel like throwing in the towel, like jumping off a bridge. People tell me that's a normal feeling, even for regular people. I don't like to blame it on my disability, but sometimes I just can't think of any other reason.

There was one time in Boston where I wrote a note. I don't think it was due to the medicine I was taking at the time, but my mom does. I think it had more to do with the fact that I can be an extremely sensitive person. When you feel ignored, or you feel that you're being neglected for no reason, you start to wonder what the hell is going on.

I was eighteen or so, spending the weekend in Boston with my brother, and my nephew and niece stopped playing with me. I thought they were pulling back from me. I felt like nobody wanted to be around me. I felt like a complete loser. So I wrote a note that said that I was retarded and felt like killing myself, that no one cared about me. I was feeling enormous self-pity, helplessness, powerlessness, depression, and anger.

I put the letter under a phone where I knew it would be found. I wanted attention. I wanted to know that people cared. My sister-in-law found it and was really upset.

I knew I was being way overdramatic. But you do that shit when you're depressed, and I definitely was. I had left the note so my brother and my sister-in-law wouldn't find it until after I left. When my sister-in-law found it, she immediately called my mother. She was so upset by it that she didn't know what to do. She told my mom, "You've got to get Quinn help."

My mom was convinced that it was the Adderall I'd just been put on, that the medicine was making me feel suicidal. They took me off of it immediately. But to me, I think the truth is that I wanted attention. It was a long time ago. When you're younger, you don't really know what you're doing. So I did everything I could to get people to notice me. And sometimes I took it to the extreme.

Nobody likes to feel ignored. Unless you're just a big-time loner, which I kind of was in high school. And I think if you're a loner, you have more of a chance of being depressed. There are a lot of "normal" people who feel depressed, for sure, but when you know that you're different, you can feel like you're dealing with more than what other people deal with.

When you're young, there's more of that than when you get older and you realize that there are other people who go through what you're going through. Being young and having any kind of disorder is hard. Anything that makes you different is hard.

Sometimes I'll see a leaf being driven over by cars, and it'll slowly get to the other side of the road. That's how I feel from time to time.

Medication

There were tons of medicines when I was a kid, to deal with my heart and all the various surgeries and seizures. I don't even really count those. Don't remember them, anyhow. The first real drug I took for my learning disabilities was Ritalin, which they put me on to try to help me focus in school. As Dr. Shprintzen would tell you, after a few years it didn't exactly agree with me all that well because kids with VCFS can have bad reactions to it. My mom was beginning to think it was making me insane. I was fine with going off of it, because right around then kids starting smashing it and snorting it. They took a lot of kids off it then.

Also, Ritalin was a new drug at the time, and they really didn't know that much about it. We were the guinea pigs. They probably should have done more research before they started prescribing it. I didn't have any better luck with Adderall—it was the worst—so they took me off of that right away, too.

The next drug my doctors put me on was Dexedrine. I was on that for a couple of years. The problem with Dexedrine was that every side effect affected me. My mouth was so dry. I had to carry a water bottle around with me, basically, and I would practically have to dump the whole thing on my lips. It wasn't attractive.

It did help me, though. It made me focus more. I've thought about going back on it. The problem is that you never get hungry at all, ever. You have no appetite. (Though I could use some of that right about now. My belly, what I like to call "my little friend," could stand a breather.)

Most kids at Gow and Landmark were on some kind of medication. At any special-needs school, you'll see that. A lot of kids are ashamed to say they're taking this or taking that, and they won't really talk about it. It's the same reason why most kids don't really compare learning disabilities, because you might feel embarrassed.

At Gow, they didn't let you keep your drugs in the room. You'd have to go get them from the school nurse. They didn't want kids with learning disabilities just sitting around in their rooms with drugs. I can understand that.

The head nurse at Gow, Rita Buckley, became like a surrogate mom to me. She was strict, but she was also so nice. No matter how sick you were, even if you had a broken leg, she'd make you go back and get a note from your dorm master. And she watched everybody take their pills every morning, made us open our mouths so she could be sure people weren't hiding them to use later.

I became very close with Rita. I knew that she would look after me. I didn't really hang out in the infirmary all the time, but every once in a while I'd fake it a little just to be able to stay there. She'd say, "If you're sick, then you can't do all these things," and it would be things I'd want to do, so I'd leave. She was great.

Aside from the ADD drugs, I've also been on and off antidepressants. Kind of a mixed bag there, too. I guess I'm like a living experimentation of what drugs are good for you.

First I took Lexipro. It takes a little while to kick in. That's the scary part, that time while you're starting. I did notice a difference right away, though. I just felt happy all the time. I didn't think about jumping off a bridge, or a gun, or anything. Depression was the last thing on my mind. But I went off of it after a while because I was gaining a lot of weight.

After that, I was on and off Effexor. It does help you concentrate a little bit, but it's more just to keep your mind proactive. The only problem with Effexor is that I gain weight while I am taking it. That's kind of an oxymoron, if you ask me. Antidepressants are supposed to make you feel good, but they make you gain weight so you feel depressed.

One of my good friends who lived in Oxford, England, committed suicide in part because she had stopped taking her medication. She was bipolar, and was very depressed. I went to her funeral. It was heartbreaking.

It's hard to know if you should be on medicine or not. Sometimes I just get tired of being on it, because I feel that it stops helping me. I went off the Effexor early last year, and I dropped almost twenty pounds and felt pretty good for a while. But then after a couple of months I noticed that my mood was pretty consistently low. I told my mom and my therapist, and we all agreed that I should try going back on the medication. I started back up in December of last year, and we'll see how it goes. It's a constant process, for all of us.

But whether I'm on the medication or not, it really does feel like my life is changing for the better. I'm becoming somebody, slowly. My whole life I've been kind of wrapped up in a cocoon, and now I'm just starting to come out. I've been a caterpillar, and now I'm turning into a butterfly. That may sound kind of dorky, but that's how it feels. That's the best way I can describe it.

The
Documentary

When I finished the year at NYFA, I decided to come back to work with Mark Muheim. Though Maryland isn't exactly the hotbed of filmmaking, I knew I could learn a lot. I started working with him three or four days a week.

Mark was a really great boss. He was very understanding of me and my needs. And he always encouraged me to keep trying to make progress. My mom says I was very lucky to be able to work with him, and I know this is true.

Right when I got there, I told Mark that for a long time I had been wanting to make a documentary about kids with learning disabilities. I had started to think about it as a film project when I was at AU, and the idea had continued to grow in my head. At film school, they said, "Stick with what you know." And learning disabilities and being different—that's something I know.

Mark helped me to make a documentary on fragile X, which is what Lisa's son Dillon has. It was hard at first, but as I started, I realized what an amazing kid Dillon is. I would interview him, and his brother Ryan. They're exactly the same in every way, and at the same time entirely different. Dillon can go into his own world. He can remember things word for word from movies about the cavalry or the army, and he's always acting out some character. He's a really sweet kid. And his brother, Ryan, is basically a genius, taking college classes at St. Mary's at thirteen.

With Mark's help, we made a short documentary about Dillon and about fragile X, which was shown at the National Fragile X Foundation conference in 2007. It gave me the idea to do a documentary on VCFS.

When I was at Landmark and first getting interested in film, I had told Dr. Shprintzen about it. He told me that he had some footage but he didn't know what to do with it. They didn't have anybody to make anything, and they couldn't really afford to put it together as a movie. So if we were willing to make a film, Dr. Shprintzen said he'd give us the tapes.

About two years ago, Mark and I went up to the SUNY Upstate Medical University in Syracuse, New York, where Dr. Shprintzen and his team run the Velo-Cardio-Facial Syndrome International Center. He moved there from the Bronx about eleven years ago.

We shot footage for a few days. That's where we got the shots of me walking through the office. You can kind of tell that I'm a little self-conscious about the stuff I'm in. I think my proper place is behind the camera or in the editing room. I'd love to be an actor, but I don't think that's in the cards for me.

Then we came back and cut the film. It's only about twelve minutes long, but it gives you all the basics on VCFS and Dr. Shprintzen and what the team he works with does. They really run an amazing place. I was really happy with how it turned out. My parents paid Mark to help me make the film, and then we donated it to the VCFS International Center's fundraising efforts at SUNY Upstate Medical University. They use it now to help them raise money for research.

As with everything in my life, even this experience wasn't perfect for me. Mark wanted me to take a shot at editing it before he and his team helped, but my editing skills weren't as good as theirs. It made more sense for them to do it.

The problem was that while Mark and his team were making the edits, I kind of felt like I wasn't really a part of it. Like I was just watching them make the film. My mom says that that's because I have a harder time working well with other people. And that I think that if I don't do everything myself, then I don't know what I'm doing.

Maybe that's true. But whatever it is, I felt like I didn't really have a part in the film. When I had an idea, they just kind of said that it would be better how they were doing it. And again, maybe they were right. Mark was always incredibly nice to me, and I know he only wanted to make the best film together that we could. He really wanted it to be my film.

I learned a lot, and it was a good experience regardless of how I felt. I'm really happy with how the whole thing turned out in the end. I don't love to watch it, but I've heard that's normal for people who do creative things. After you've gone through the process of sweating it out, watching it can bring back memories of what you went through. Kind of gives you an icky feeling.

I think it's a good film for VCFS, though. I hope it can help them raise money and raise awareness. I'm happy to have done it and proud of it, and I'm excited for *you* to watch it. That's all that really matters.

Independence

To me, independence is the scariest word in the English language. It's like sex, in a way. You're very curious about it. And you don't really know what it is until you experience it.

Independence is big for me. It's one of my biggest issues. Every therapist I've ever been to has always wanted to talk about my issues with independence the most. I do want to be independent, but I also sort of don't want to. The same is true of my mom. She wants me to be independent, but she doesn't want it at the same time. In truth, I think we're both a little bit afraid of it.

It's hard to know what's realistic to expect for me sometimes, and independence is no different. That's where Dr. Shprintzen can be helpful. He can explain the things that I can't.

Dr. Shprintzen
Most families of patients with VCFS struggle with the idea of independence. Will I have to take care of my child for the

rest of his or her life? I think, in part, it depends on how you define independence. But for at least the majority of the people—I don't know the size of the majority—is a relatively typical life possible? Again, I don't use the word "normal." Is a fairly typical life possible for these people? The answer is yes. But we make accommodations in our lives all of the time.

In general, people with VCFS do well with routines. It helps to be surrounded by a loving and warm family that defines any job relative to what they know their child's capabilities are—but what they do is important. And it's appreciated. They're given work that they can do, and when they do it successfully the people around them are grateful for it. Those kinds of models can exist in all kinds of environments, but I do think something like a farm environment actually is a terrific environment for somebody with VCFS. It restricts your human contact, in terms of both criticism and expectations. There are not many different ways that you can feed a cow, but if you do it well, your farm is successful. The bottom line, though, is that whatever the setting is, kids with VCFS need to have predictability. They do not perform well when unexpected things happen.

As a last note, as with all things, expectations are key here. People with VCFS have good computer skills, often good music skills, and often good artistic skills. If somebody said, "Well, you've got great computer skills, let's look for something for you to do to work with computers," their first response might be, "Well, yeah, I'd like to go work for Bill Gates and write software for Microsoft." (Believe me, I've heard that before.) Versus something in the computer

*field that not only would be more realistic for somebody
with VCFS, but would be more realistic for anybody.*

*But if you have unrealistic expectations because of
your level of maturity, then you're going to be disappointed
unless you have people around you, like your parents, who
can guide you in the appropriate direction and let you
achieve at a level that is commensurate with your skills.
Everybody's got to do something, and the corollary is that
there's a place for everybody. It's just an issue of being realistic, and of finding that place.*

*   *   *

After I left the New York Film Academy, I lived at
home in Georgetown for a while. In September
2007, I moved into the house next door to my parents' house with a bunch of roommates. I live in
my own place, but I'm literally next door to my parents' house and can go there whenever I want.
Sometimes the free food is kind of tough to skip.

But it's more than that. The only way for me to
truly be independent is to live on my own. I fantasize
a lot about moving to California, or someplace like
that, where I'd be able to surf all the time. I'd be
away from my parents, which I've never really been
before, with a few exceptions. But then I wonder if
I could handle that. I don't really know. Maybe a
small transition, out of their house and into the
house next door, is what I actually needed.

I think everybody knows it's going to take a little
bit of extra time for me. I can't just be independent

all of a sudden. Part of it is because of my disability, but the truth is that nobody ever really taught me the skills I would need to be independent. My mom wants me to be independent, but then she's afraid for me. I've relied on her for everything for so long that it's hard to just stop. When somebody has been taking care of you for most of your life, it's hard to break away.

In some ways, my life has been the opposite of most kids'. Because I was so sick, I was much closer to my parents in my early years, because I *had* to be. And now I'm just breaking off from my parents at twenty-six, which is a time when a lot of other kids are just starting to come back.

And when I say I'm a rich prick, it's easy to say, "Oh, he doesn't mean that," or whatever. But it's true. I was pretty spoiled. Ever since I was a little kid, I've had people doing things for me. It is taking me a while to get used to having to do them myself now. Subconsciously I guess I just kind of make people do things for me. It's kind of hard to complain about it, even if I want it to be different.

The truth is that I'm not really prepared to be independent. For one, my financial skills, on a rate from 1 to 10, are at about a 1. It's something I want to work on, because my parents aren't going to be around forever. But right now they basically take care of all of that for me. My dad has always said that I don't really know much about money, that I don't really care about it. And it's been true up to now. But even if I wanted to, I'm not sure I'll ever really be able to balance a checkbook. (Dr. Shprintzen says this is true of a lot more people than just me.)

I do know that money doesn't grow on trees. But sometimes it grows on family trees. Money does strange things to people. Including people in my family. The small lessons I'm learning now about money and how to pay my bills and stuff, I feel that all my friends learned when they were sixteen years old. I feel way behind the curve.

As far as true independence from my parents goes, my dad's not really the issue. He gives me shit about money, or some dad stuff about how I should be working harder. He sometimes thinks the ideas I have are unrealistic, but at this point I'm pretty used to that. I don't really take it personally.

It's my mom who is more involved in the day-to-day. When I think of independence, it's her I think about getting away from. Small things, and big things, too. Like if I want to go to my therapist once a week but she wants me to go twice, we will butt our heads quite a bit. That's been happening lately. If my mom had it her way, I'd probably go every day. It's like, "Mom, I'm not *that* fucked up."

And, obviously, she's always a little terrified for me. I'm her only child. And I've got these problems that she wants to help me with, always help me with. My whole life, she's been the one who saves me. She'll probably be terrified for me even after she's dead. She'll haunt my ass.

My mom, my archangel.

She's a very powerful woman. She's like a lioness. You don't want to mess with her. She has controlled a lot of my life. Sometimes I'm angry about that, because I feel I'm in the passenger seat of the car and I have to ride wherever the driver wants me to go. Sometimes I feel as if I have no freedom.

There's a documentary film called *Grey Gardens* about a crazy mother and daughter, Little Edie and Big Edie, who live in this big house in the Hamptons that's falling down, with all their cats and a bunch of raccoons. The police try to evict them, but they stay. They once were really wealthy, from Jackie Kennedy's family, but they let it all go to hell. They were both pretty nuts.

Grey Gardens

My parents bought the actual house of Grey Gardens about thirty years ago, so that's where we go for the summer. It was a wreck, and they fixed it up. But sometimes I think more about Grey Gardens when I'm in D.C. In the documentary, Little Edie is always talking about how she wants to leave, but she never does. If I stay in this house for the rest of my life, I wonder if my mom and I wouldn't end up just like Little Edie and Big Edie, slowly going crazy together. We joke about it all the time.

But there is a flip side to everything. And there is truth in everything that we say. I couldn't have lived without my mom. She's saved my ass a million times. She has been like an archangel to me. She had the wings that I didn't. And she's basically carried me everywhere I've been.

If it weren't for both of my parents, I would have a much harder time. I don't mean my parents' money. I mean their love and attention. It's because of my parents that I don't put myself down every day.

Do I want to be independent of them? Yes. Will I ever be truly independent of them? I don't know. It's one of the biggest riddles of my existence.

Girls

The second biggest riddle of my existence? Girls. No question. More than anything, I really want a girlfriend. I think one of the reasons I have a hard time taking it to the next level with girls is because I had no contact with girls for much of growing up.

That may be a good thing, because it toughens you up, but in the long run, if you're straight, it sucks. Because you're going to want to get laid, which is the truth, and there's no other way to explain it. And I'm miserable, basically, because of it. It may sound funny, but I think part of my depression is that I can't get laid.

I don't know why, but I seem to have the worst luck with women, no matter how hard I try. My best friend, Stephen, says that it's not luck, that it has more to do with knowledge than anything else. If that's the case, then I guess I don't have a lot of knowledge about women. I feel that they are picking up some vibe from me that says I can't handle a relationship, or I'm not mature enough to be in a relationship. That's what Lisa tells me, anyway.

Whatever it is, I am apparently doing something wrong. I've taken and followed all of the advice that my friends and my parents have given me about dating, but it hasn't quite worked out for me yet. I may not know much about the female way of thinking, but I do know that if I were ever in a relationship, I would do everything I knew how to please the lucky lady. And I know that the key to a girl's heart is respect.

The only women I knew growing up were my mom's friends. All my mother's girlfriends are these gorgeous older women. My mom would have parties, and all her male friends would bring over their wives or girlfriends. And to me, that's just what I thought was normal. I've been attracted to older women, in part because they've been what I've known.

My biggest crush is on Katharine Weymouth, Kay Graham's granddaughter. She's the publisher

Katharine Weymouth, girl of my dreams.

and media chief of the *Washington Post* now. I have known her for a long time but spent some time with her at one of my mom's parties about five years ago. I just about fell in love with her on the spot.

I wanted to ask her out on a date, but my mom wouldn't let me. She says that I'm too young, and that Katharine is much older than I am and has three kids. I reminded her of Ashton Kutcher and Demi Moore. I'm joking, but only kind of. Where there's a will, there's a way. Maybe in my next life.

I guess, in some ways, having crushes on older women prepared me for now. It wasn't really good for me when I was younger, but it prepped me, and I learned at a young age how to please an older woman. I knew what they liked and what they didn't like. Very different from young women. Young women's minds are constantly changing and moving, figuring out what they want and don't want.

I have trouble with reading cues. I can never tell if girls like me sexually. If you're having an intimate friendly conversation and a woman is smiling and you're making her laugh, then you think that maybe it's possible to take it to the next level. But typically, the day after that kind of thing would happen with a girl, I wouldn't hear back from her. I would immediately think that I had done something wrong. Then I'd spend the rest of the day trying to figure out what it was, when most likely I hadn't even done anything wrong in the first place.

Being uneasy around girls and unsure of where I stood sometimes led me to call or text them every other minute, which didn't help my cause. I guess I was acting like a stalker, but in my mind I was just worried. It's always been hard for me.

Some of it has changed since I moved into the new house. Stephen used to live on the second floor with me, with our friends Pamela and Lindsey upstairs from us and Amy downstairs. I've learned more about women in the past year than I've known in my whole life. For one thing, I've learned that if you say you don't like their hairstyle or something, you're screwed. You are *screwed.* And never joke about their weight. Generally, though, women are a powerful breed. They're strong. You don't mess with them.

I've also learned a little more about myself. One time, I went down to Porto Bello with a few of my roommates and their boyfriends, who are really nice guys. But I didn't have anybody with me. It was fun at first, but then after watching them for a while I just started to feel depressed and bad about myself. I didn't behave all that well.

The same thing happened on a trip to New York, where I was with Stephen and his girlfriend. I got a little jealous of him spending time with his girlfriend instead of me. The great thing about Stephen is that he's my best friend in the world, so when I get upset he listens to me and talks to me about things, instead of getting upset, too. We're able to work through it.

I think when people get jealous about something they tend to imagine things, because they don't want the situation they're faced with to be true (even though they know that it is). They will find something else to blame it on, so they don't have to blame it on themselves. I think that's what I was doing in that situation.

The one problem with having pretty women living with you is that you can't really do anything about it. You've got to keep your zipper zipped, if you know what I mean. But I try to look at the bright side.

Sometimes it's easy for me to think the worst of myself, that I'm a loser, that I'll never find a girlfriend, that I'll be a nobody for the rest of my life. I still do that sometimes, but I'm getting better at not beating myself up about such a little thing. I try to remind myself that there are much worse situations to be in. But still, I'd love for it to change.

I'm a late bloomer. Girls don't really figure out they want nice guys until they're, like, thirty. And if all else fails, I could always pull a Gauguin and take one of my nieces' cute teenage friends down to Tahiti with me. (Joke.)

How It Feels,
Take Three

People always want to know what it "feels like" to have VCFS, or to be learning disabled. It's hard for me to answer, because my life is my life, and it's hard to know what's normal for me that's normal for other people and what's normal for me that isn't normal for other people. What's normal?

I have a really hard time finding things. Like on my NOLS trip, or even when my mom says, "It's in the fridge," and then I go to look for it, and I look around and around and around and can't find it. And then she'll come, and it'll be right there in front of my face. That bothers me a lot. But it may also be genetic. I mean, my dad can't find shit. He's always losing his keys. So it's hard to know.

One of the hardest things for me is when people are asking me to do different things all at once, like three different people and five different things. It's confusing, and it stresses me out. That was one of the reasons I left college, because my work was just getting me so stressed out. Keeping up with a lot of different demands from different places overwhelms my head sometimes. I can't function.

Reading is another obvious place where it gets a little funky for me. It's not that I can't read the words. The problem is that I have to translate what I'm reading into a language my brain will understand. It's like translating from French to calculus. Maybe it's weird that it takes me so long to read, but it doesn't embarrass me. It's just a curiosity.

The truth is that my brain works differently every day. There are really good days and really bad days, and everything in between. But in a way that's what I like about my disability. It's interesting. I don't know how my brain's going to work when I get up in the morning. It's unpredictable. One thing I can tell you is that if I don't get enough sleep, my brain doesn't work at all.

It's like living in another world. I have a hard time remembering the days of the week, or the order of the months of the year. But you see some things maybe more clearly than other people. I always try to keep my mind occupied on other things, not thinking, well, you know, "I'm learning disabled, I might as well not try." I always give everything my best shot.

But it's true that my sense of direction is pretty screwed up. I get lost really easily, just kind of turned around. Whenever my friends will come in from out of town, I feel bad telling them, "I can't pick you up from the airport." Even though I have a navigation system in the car, I'm so afraid of getting lost.

My friends probably think I sound like some lazy kid who won't come get them, but it's not that I don't want to. I would love to pick them up. But I'm just terrified of it.

My dad has a little trouble with his sense of direction, too. One time we got on the wrong train in New York, going the wrong way. My dad isn't learning disabled. So how do you explain that?

Over the years, I've gotten more used to it. When I was little and I would get lost, I would kind of freak out. Now I know how to use a navigation system, and can usually figure out where I am. I also realized that I can ask for help. I can drive down to Porto Bello without any problem. It's an hour and a half away, but I don't even think about it. It's so instinctive, I couldn't even tell somebody how to get down there.

Socially, I know I have a hard time reading cues. So when I go out, I study people. How they walk, how they act around other people. I observe everything, so I can learn how to be as normal as possible.

This has always been a racist country, though I hope that will change now that Obama will be president. Sometimes, if you're black and you go into a white church, or a room that's predominantly white, everybody's going to stare at you. That's what it feels like to be me sometimes. Even though you can't really point your finger at it, you just feel it.

If I go out with friends, with people who know me, other people will have less of a chance to figure it out. It's sort of like how wolves travel in packs.

I'm a lone wolf. And that's what I am, most of the time. I'm always trying to find a pack to be with.

Sometimes I want to be more like a hawk. Hawks are different from any other birds, and I think other birds might be jealous of the hawk, because it's fierce and it can survive on its own. But at the same time, a hawk can't fit in with any other bird. I think there are connections between people and Mother Nature.

It was hard for me sometimes when I was a kid, but there were only a few people who ever looked at me like I was from Mars. There is still—and I think there always will be—a tiny, tiny little prick of fear when I'm asking a question. I don't think that'll ever go away. But I'll be able to practice at it. Before I order something at a restaurant, I always practice saying the order in my head. It's just something that I automatically do, so I don't screw up.

In the end for me it comes down to reading cues, and wondering what's normal and what's not. It's kind of like a box you can never think your way out of. So I just have to trust things more, and maybe relax a little. People tell me sometimes I need to take some things less seriously. I think getting laid would definitely help in that department.

Anybody who really knows me knows that I'm obsessed with nice cars. Ferraris, Lamborghinis, all of them. Ever since I was a little kid. That could be further proof that I'm a spoiled rich kid. But it's not like I have one. I just like to learn about them—

though of course I want one. (A Lamborghini Reventón. They only made twenty of them.) But I'm not the only one. Dr. Shprintzen loves fast cars, too. He has a big collection of model Ferraris on his desk.

Everybody always says those nice cars are over the top, or too much. I've always felt that I've been too little. I've never been enough for people. My liking those cars is like somebody shy meeting somebody who's really outgoing and being completely blown away.

It's the same reason that sometimes I've been attracted to fast girls. In some ways it's a rebellion against my mom, because she's so nice and pretty. But most of it is that I was so slow growing up. I've always been behind. I figure if I meet a fast girl, she might whip me into shape a little bit. Get me up to speed.

I feel like I've always been this prissy little Goody Two-shoes who does everything the right way. But I love Lamborghinis and Ferraris because I want to go fast. When I see a Lamborghini, I see pure freedom. You can go as fast as you want.

Advocacy

What's "normal" for me isn't normal for other people. Even people with VCFS. I was lucky to be born into my family. At least when I'm in Washington, I always feel like everybody knows who my parents are. And also, my parents had the resources to be able to send me to the finest schools, and hire me tutors, and my mom didn't have to work so she could sit with me in the hospital when I was sick as a kid. The list goes on. Not every family has as much time to devote to a special kid, and my mom and dad and I all know that and are grateful for it.

Because of who my parents are, I've gone on some really nice adventures, to the Caribbean and Ireland and even South Africa, where I got to meet Nelson Mandela. We went to where he was imprisoned on Robben Island and everything. He was the nicest man I've ever met. He had been told about all of the problems I had faced in my life, and he said to me, "Quinn, I am honored to meet you." He also

Meeting Nelson Mandela in South Africa.

put his arm on my shoulder. That was one of the greatest moments of my life.

I've had a lot of opportunities that other kids don't have. Sometimes I have been taken advantage of as a result, but mostly I've benefited. Your regular kid wouldn't be getting book deals and hiring writing partners.

There have been other things that I've gotten to do because of who my parents are. For whatever reason, I go to a lot of events where there's some chance to speak, and people always seem to want me to do it.

Some are obvious, like when my grandparents died. My grandfather died on September 11, 2000. That was a big day for me. I loved my grandfather so much. I was afraid to speak, but I was doing it for my mom, and for my grandfather. I wore my kilt in honor of his Scotch-Irish ancestry. Also, I think wearing a kilt allows you to express yourself in a different way. That there's a completely different person inside of you.

I wrote something out before my grandfather's funeral, but I didn't use it. (My dad can never believe that I speak without notes.) Justin told me that people remember 30 percent more when they take notes. So sometimes, because I have a hard time reading, I'll write out my thoughts beforehand, but when I get up there to speak I'll remember what I wanted to say without having to read it. According to everybody who was at my grandfather's funeral, I did a good job.

I also had to give a speech at Children's Hospital, in 1999, because they were naming the radiology unit after me. It was partly because I basically lived in that hospital when I was a kid, and partly because my mom and dad helped raise a lot of money for them.

My speech was about how life is a maze. Not just for LD kids, but for everybody. You've got to find your way out. You may run into a bunch of walls. Or you might be at a point where you think you're doing really well, you're really going and you're on a roll, but right when you think you've got it, you come upon another wall. There are things that are just hard. Hard courses, hard everything. But hard can turn into great if you stick with it and look at it right. So you have to change directions and find another way to the end of the maze. Children's Hospital helped me through my own maze.

A few years later, when I was at Gow, there was a big LD conference at the Hilton Hotel in New York City. My parents and I were all supposed to speak, because it was about how learning disabilities affect the whole family. My headmaster from Gow met us, and he helped me talk through what I was going to say. It was basically the maze speech again.

The only difference this time was that they told me 250 people were going to be there, so I was already a little bit nervous. Then I walked in, and there were about 650 people.

When I stood up, I was really nervous. My throat was in my heart. I couldn't hold my speech straight, and my hands were shaking. I spoke maybe three minutes.

I don't love public speaking. I don't think my dad does, either. Every time there's a speech, I really don't want to do it, but at the end I always feel good about myself. It builds up my confidence, and it helps other people. It helps kids, but it also helps parents to know that having a kid like me isn't the end of the world.

I was at the LD conference because I have a learning disability. I was pretty much the representative of all those kids. So I just tried to be myself.

It went really well. After the speech was over, a guy from the University of Arizona (where they have a school for special education) came up to invite me to Arizona. He said he could train me in public speaking, and we could go around the country giving speeches. It was flattering. I must have done a good job. We celebrated that night with some champagne back at the hotel.

I've never seen my mom so happy in her life. There have been a lot of rough moments in my life, so I think the sweet ones are that much sweeter for my parents. This is what my mom says about when she was proudest of me, both before this night and on this night:

One of the most gratifying moments was at the graduation ceremony at Gow at the end of Quinn's freshman year. He wore his kilt. That's the really interesting thing about Quinn. I mean, he is a very individual person. He is his own person. And he isn't going to change or be something else in order to fit in or get along with the crowd. He's not going to be a weirdo; he's just got his own thing.

But he stood up there in his kilt, and he got two prizes. He won the math prize, and then he won the Browning Prize, which is the prize you get for having the most determination and true grit and all that. He won it two years in a row. But that freshman year, at the end of the freshman year, when he won those two prizes, I just thought, you know, this is worth all the agony, because he really did it. He really did it.

We always try to be "realistic" about Quinn and whatever his limitations might be, but it's hard because he often surprises you. You think you're being realistic and then it turns out that in fact he could do something that you never expected him to do.

Quinn wrote the speech that he gave at the Hilton by himself, and he stood up and gave it, and he got a standing ovation. People were crying. I think that may have been the happiest moment of my life, that night. I mean, he got up in front of 600 people and gave this incredibly brilliant speech and got a standing ovation and he was mobbed for an hour afterward. People kept coming up to him and asking him to come out and speak to their groups. The editor of the learning disorder magazine got the speech and printed it.

It was just, I was over the moon. I mean, I can't really describe the feeling of complete ecstasy that I felt that night. We went back to the hotel, and I didn't want to go to bed, so we went into the bar and had some champagne. Quinn had a glass, and we toasted him. I remember feeling like I was almost levitating, I was so proud. If you talk about the happiest moments of my life, the day he was born and that day were two really happy moments. Because I looked at him that night, and I thought, "You know what? He's really going to make it."

My mother was a really magical person. She was somebody people were just automatically drawn to, just this incredible way about her. And I've told Quinn that my mother had the magic, and that he has the magic, too. That he has the magic from my mother. So he's always believed that he has the magic, you know? And I think that's true. I think he does.

Only once has Quinn ever said, "Why me?" It was when he was about twenty-one, and he asked me that. And I said, "Why not you?" I could spend a lot of time asking the same questions about my own life; to some extent, all of us could. But I believe that he was put here for a reason, and that reason is to do good, and to help other people. Everything is material, so use it. This is what you've been given, and let's look at it as a gift. That's "why you." And I think Quinn is truly starting to believe that, too.

You can see it in what he's doing with his Web site now. He blogs almost every single day, and he absolutely loves it. When he was a child, I think he felt intimidated by what Ben and I did, and he never seemed to have any interest in writing or jounalism at all. But now that he's got a purpose to his work, and he's writing for—and about—other people like himself, everything has changed.

The other day, he said to me, "Mom, maybe I am a writer after all."

And it's working for him because he is speaking from his heart, and he's using his own life, his own experiences, to try to help other people. It's sort of like a continuation of what he did that night at the Hilton. I'm just so proud of him.

Web Site
and Book

———

Looking back, I think that the VCFS film I made with Mark was a continuation of the speech I gave at the LD conference. When we had viewing parties for the film in D.C. and New York, I had to give a little talk about it afterwards. I realized that I'm getting more and more comfortable doing things like that. It's kind of second nature now. I went by myself to Texas for the VCFS Educational Foundation annual meeting in 2007 and introduced the film there, too—one of my first trips like that by myself in my life.

My dream life would be to make documentaries, and eventually feature films. For now, what I know is my life, my family, and my story. Telling that story is enough for the time being, and I hope that the film can help people. Even though I've seen it so many times that I'm kind of tired of watching it myself, it is out there every day doing good for VCFS.

When I started to think about the jobs that I'd had up to this point, I realized that none of them had ever really fit me right. What fits me is feeling like I'm doing something for other people.

Because of where I come from, I have had the opportunity to make speeches and movies, and to travel around talking. I got this book deal. Maybe *that's* my place, or at least a part of my place. Maybe working for other people, or raising awareness about VCFS, is better than worrying about myself. I'd love to make feature films in Hollywood. But working for other kids like me is something that I know I can do.

I first got the deal for this book when I was eighteen. We were going to trace my journey into manhood. I think maybe it was a little premature at the time. We ultimately decided not to go through with it then.

I'm twenty-six now, and I've changed a lot from my eighteen-year-old self. Then, I thought maybe I might go to a "normal" four-year college, that even Harvard wasn't out of the question. Now, I'm pretty sure my schooling days are over, but you never know. In the deck of cards of life, I've won some and lost some. That's the real story, not that I rode off into the shining sunset or anything.

One day when we were driving down to Porto Bello, I said to my folks that a lot of people who are successful start out on the Internet. My first idea was for a genealogical Web site, because genealogy is something I've been passionate about for as long as I can remember. But I realized that there are so many genealogical Web sites out there, it's ridiculous. My dad agreed.

When I started thinking seriously, I just thought that there's got to be something that needs to be done that nobody's ever done. Coming up with ideas is really hard. But that's one of the good things about being ADD: We generate a lot of ideas.

Eventually I came up with the idea for a social networking site for kids with learning disabilities and VCFS and other problems, a place where kids from all over the world could talk to each other. It was the kind of thing I would use. I knew about Facebook but hadn't used it yet. What I had in my mind was different.

My mom loved the idea. But then, of course, my dad had a different reaction. My dad is the kind of guy who always says, "Well, who's going to pay for it?" You know, "Where are you going to get the money from?" Whenever I come up with ideas for documentaries, my dad will always say, "You've got to do the research." He's sure that there's already a documentary about it, whatever it is. So he's telling me, "Do research on it, see if it's been done before. Then come back and talk to me."

The more we thought about it, the more it seemed like a good idea. We met with some people in New York, a place that did a bunch of Web sites for magazines, but it would have cost us too much money to develop it, so that didn't work. Then we met with Chris Schroeder and his team at Health Central.com. Chris did www.washingtonpost.com, so you know he's not a slacker. He and his team loved the idea, and we built the site over the last year.

It's called Friends of Quinn, at www.Friends OfQuinn.com, and it's a social networking site for kids who have all kinds of learning disabilities. It has some of the best features of Facebook and YouTube, but it's geared toward people like me— people with learning disabilities and certain genetic syndromes. Most important, it will be a place where people can go when they wonder, "Is this normal?" It will help people answer that question and feel less alone.

One of the things I don't like about Facebook is that you can add a person as your "favorite friend." And all my friends have added them, and I'm nobody's favorite friend. That kind of sucks. I don't like favoritism. All it does is make some people feel good, and other people feel bad. I used to see it in high school all the time. I don't want to have that happen to anybody on this site.

Some of the features on Facebook and sites like it are hard for me to use. Figuring out how to upload a picture on Facebook was really hard for me. On our site, we're doing our best to make it all simpler and easier. You'll be able to upload pictures and videos with one or two clicks and ask questions of medical experts and the whole community. There are resources for parents and brothers and sisters, too.

Everybody who's working on the Web site thinks that it already fills a real need. There's nothing quite like it out there. In my biggest dream, the site can be a call to action for the whole LD community, to get people involved and connected.

One of the best things about developing the site is that it has now become my full-time job. I've never had one before. I work in the HealthCentral offices every day, from ten in the morning until four in the afternoon. I write blogs almost every day, and I help out in every way that I can. The truth is, I can't wait to get to work in the morning. And I'm not just saying that. I love working on the site, and I really like the people who work there. We spend a lot of time laughing and joking, and I just feel so lucky to be there.

And also, it feels like a real first step toward independence. I have to figure out how to manage my salary, deal with a real boss, and all the rest of it. Nothing happens all at once, and I still need help with things, but sometimes the first step is the most important one.

I hope to be working on the Web site for a long time, reaching out to other kids like me. I also want to shoot short videos of people talking about their disabilities to post on the site. (I've shot a few things like that already for my mom's Web site at the *Washington Post*, "On Faith," which has given me some good practice.) If that is of service, then I will have done my job.

I've already had people say to me, "Well, you're only developing this Web site because of who your parents are." To some extent, that's true. I'm sure people like working with Ben Bradlee and Sally Quinn.

Sometimes it's hard for me to know if something is happening because of my mom or my dad, or because of me. I think about that a lot. And if it's happening only because of my mom or dad, I sort of wish it *wouldn't*. It's really hard to know.

In the end, I can't control any of that. And it's always been that way for me. The real question isn't about my parents. The real question is: Is this site fun, and does it work well? Will it do some good for other people like me?

If the answer is yes, then I think I've done what I'm supposed to do, regardless of how the door got opened. Doors open for you for strange reasons. You don't need to stop and say, "What's the real reason this door opened?" You just walk through the door and then face what you face on the other side. That's what I aspire to. Finding out what's on the other side of the door.

The
Future

With my Web site and this book, I feel like I've turned the corner. I feel like my life is on the upswing. I remember at the stroke of New Year's this last year, I thought, "This will be my year. This will be when it all works out." I hope that's true.

Right after the new year started, I went down to Porto Bello with my parents and some of our friends. When I was born, Edward Bennett Williams and Art Buchwald and Nora Ephron and Ann Pincus were my godparents. Edward Bennett Williams and Art Buchwald are dead now, and I know my dad misses them both even more than I do.

Ann and Nora will always be my primary godparents, and I love them both. But they're my mom's age, and I told my parents that I thought it might be a good idea to add some newer godparents. My parents are so much older than I am. I wanted to choose people who live in D.C. and are part of a younger generation. We decided that we would have a re-christening ceremony down at Porto Bello, my favorite place in the world.

It might seem like a strange thing to have done. The Episcopal priest who performed the ceremony, a nice guy named Jim Anderson, said that he'd never heard of it before. But we did it because I know I'm going to need some help from adults from time to time in my life. Not direct help—I don't need to live with them, or anything—just help. I sometimes need help navigating the world. (Sometimes I fantasize about being a pirate, or some other kind of expert navigator, who always knows where they're going.)

My dad is eighty-seven years old. I've been thinking a lot about him not being here. One of the last times we were out working together in the woods, he said, "I'm just getting so clumsy and old." He's not one who would say something like that. He didn't say it to me—he just sort of said it out loud, to himself, maybe.

My dad was also really close with his dad. One of the reasons I like to go to my parents' house for breakfast isn't because I can't be independent or can't make my own breakfast. It's because I know my time with my dad is limited. I don't really have a brother I'm close to. He's the only thing I've got besides my mom. When we're together, we're like little kids, always horsing around.

My only regret is that I'm hard on my dad sometimes. I constantly remind him of the mistakes that he makes. Truthfully, I don't think I'm trying to hurt him. It's just my way of dealing with what's happening. I think I have a hard time forgiving my dad for getting old. I'm mad at time. I don't want time to pass, at least in terms of what's in store for my father. People aren't invincible, and he's in the winter of his life.

In some ways lately, I'm taking my dad's place. In the woods I do more of the heavy lifting now. And I don't really let him do much with the chainsaw anymore, either. Up till a few years ago, he'd even pick up an ax to chop the wood. A guy in his eighties, chopping wood with an ax. I took it away from him, finally.

My mom will be around forever, one way or another. But my dad won't be. I know how lucky I am to have this relationship with him. I remember being little and going to spend the night at a friend's house, and he said good night without hugging his parents. I thought that was the weirdest thing. I realized that I had an unusual relationship with both of my parents, a very close one. Maybe what will motivate me going forward is wanting to make my dad proud of me. Even when he isn't here anymore, I don't want to let him down.

My dad isn't one to sit on the couch and psychoanalyze things, but I know he thinks about this stuff, too. I'm different from his other kids, and he's had to figure out how to handle that just like I have. You've heard from my mom a few times, but not

Enjoying a ride on my dad's shoulders.

from my dad yet, and I wanted to give him a chance to talk about what it's been like for him to live with me up to now. Here is how he puts it:

When we had Quinn, I had ten years to go as editor. But even still, I had so much more time to devote to Quinn. I thank God, because he was a child who needed that time—the parental time, the paternal time. He's made me so much more aware of the importance that all of our frail-

ties have in forming our characters. That it isn't just about successes. It's about so much more. I've gotten more pleasure out of smaller Quinn triumphs than I've gotten out of other big triumphs. This wouldn't have been true with my other kids.

In terms of our family unit, Quinn is the overwhelming subject of our relationship. That's what our life is, is Quinn. It's never been true for me in earlier children. I mean, it was always fun to have a child and be preoccupied with having a child, but it isn't anything like what it is now.

In the first place, I was climbing up the ladder, working hard, working late, with endless hours. And in my previous marriage, there were six children, all told. To divide yourself into six is awfully tough, and makes the time you spend with each one child much less. I feel lucky to have had so much time to give to Quinn, from working in the woods together on down.

My polio, which I sort of belittled as I was living through it, was mainly a much more important thing to me than I remembered because I got through it. I never doubted it. That's what the shrinks all got so excited about. But I don't say to myself, "Oh, I know what Quinn's going through." The only real similarity is the confrontation of a child with a physical problem. I've always had the great belief in curability. That things will get fixed, or that you can fix things. That hasn't been true of Quinn.

The image I will never lose of Quinn is when he was in that plastic tent, three months old, just after the operation. Sally was on one side and I was on the other, and we had a finger through the thing and he had a finger in each hand. The way he held on when he was so young, and he couldn't talk. He was out. But he just held on. Held on. He kept going.

We have a famous expression in my family, that my father used to say to me—or, at least, I tell it like my father said it to me. "Nose down, ass up, and push forward." That's what you do. You keep trying. It's very primitive. It's not all that intellectual. But I never had to fight like Quinn did, when I had polio. I think I cried once over the frustration of polio, that I couldn't do something. But I was much older. I was fourteen, already in a position to articulate things.

Quinn can be so surprising. There is so much that he understands, but sometimes he can find it difficult to cope. He's confounded when he's lost. He doesn't know how to regroup. There are times when I've gotten discouraged with that. So much of scrambling, of surviving, is improvising. I don't know how good he is at that either. He has talked over the years about being called a retard by pals at school, way back. I can see why people say that, because nobody knew what his syndrome was and there are certain things he doesn't process well. The flip side of it is that his triumphs are real triumphs.

I've watched as he recognized that he was different—how he ascertains it, explores it, and then how he copes with that. At some point, you have to reach an understanding of your limitations, to stop fooling yourself, to cope and to fight back. What methods do you use to do it? How does he overcome those difficulties? There's the instinct to overcome in that child that's just overpowering.

I'm not sure I know how Quinn's brain works. I know that at certain times, Quinn's brain doesn't act in a way that we think is logical. Sometimes his answers and sometimes his observations seem inappropriate. You have to spend time thinking about how he got there. Usually I can work out a logic to it. You see what path he took to get there, and what seemed to be inappropriate isn't. But sometimes other people don't get it. In school he didn't know his roommate's last names. I'm not sure how you explain that.

I've always pushed Quinn. "Let him do it himself, let him work it out. He's got to learn how to do this." And Sally is sometimes reluctant to come down that path, and is often more ready to bail him out. That must be wonderful from Quinn's point of view, but I don't know where it leaves him. Sally is fierce. I think a lot of people realize that you just don't really mess with Sally Quinn, because it's not worth it. But I do think more and more it's good for him to get out on his own and start coping with some of life's problems without having Sally on his shoulder.

My big worry with any book like this is that his whole life, Quinn has felt like his mother and I are out front and center, giving speeches, all that kind of thing. We were both too far out front sometimes. I think that prevented him from fading into the woodwork, which was what he was trying to do probably. Sally and I are a part of this, but this is Quinn's book. We're not front and center. We're just part of the story. I think he is used to disappearing when we show up. That can't be true here.

I'm nervous about where Quinn will find a community that he can be a really good contributing part of. It doesn't have to be the same big community as his parents have chosen. It can be a really small community. I feel that he goes through life with us at his side. He's in great shape, and we can bail him out. But we've got to get him past that.

Ultimately, I want him to be safe, and I want him to find a way to become a productive member of society without us. And luckily, because of the age difference, if we're lucky Sally's going to be around for a long time. I think a lot about the fact that I'm sixty years older than he is; I really do. But hopefully in another twenty years or so, long after I'm gone, we'll have found a place for him, and he'll have found a place for himself. There's only so much we can do, in the end. You can get things set, but they only stay set for so long.

Sometimes I wonder, are we putting obstacles in his way or are we actually helping him in the long term? It's impossible to know sometimes. I do know that Quinn is a charming kid with more to offer the world than standardized testing would tell you. I don't know where he will end up. I've had a wonderful run in my life, but there isn't much more I can do. I love him with all my heart.

This past January, I added four new godparents to help me out as time goes on: Kyle Gibson, Lisa Kelley, David Ignatius, and Angus Yates. All good friends.

You've heard a lot about Lisa, but Kyle is also really important to me. She worked on this book with me for a while, and she is a great friend. She's also the hottest fifty-year-old woman you'd ever hope to see. She's always there for me, and we have a lot of fun hanging out. I spent election night with her this past November, and we watched Obama's speech and then went down near the White House to see everybody going crazy. (Obama is the man.) Kyle always listens to me, always makes me feel better, and I'm so happy to have her as one of my new godmothers.

David is a great family friend, with the added benefit of having three beautiful daughters. And Angus is another very close friend. He was friends with my half brother Dino, and for the first twelve years of my life, I thought he was literally my brother. No joke. I should have figured it out, given that he's blond and about six foot four, but I didn't.

Everybody came down to the farm one Saturday for the ceremony. My parents and I went down Friday, and I think the ghosts of Porto Bello came out to say hi. We joked, because the power goes off a lot down there, probably because it's just an old house. Or some drunk-ass kid hit a telephone pole.

We had just finished dinner, and my mom was doing the seating for the next day when the power went off. My mom would have to be blind not to do the seating. She did the seating without power, without anything. She did it by candlelight. If my dad and I are going to the Brome Howard, my mom will actually tell us where to sit, on which side of the table to sit. She loves to figure out the seating. It's like her Sudoku. (If you really want to learn her tactics, you should buy her book, *The Party*. You're welcome, mom.)

The next day, everybody came down, we had dinner, and on Sunday morning we had about a half-hour ceremony at the Brome Howard. I got sick the night before, during the night, which wasn't ideal, but it worked out okay. All of my new godparents stood with me and gave pledges to be there for me.

At the end, I raised a glass for a toast. I said to them, "I give you this glass, from the place that I love so dearly." And then it was done. Four new godparents. They all seemed to get along great. I think it makes my parents happy to know that there will be people around who care about me and love me and will help take care of me when they're gone.

As far as what the future holds, I don't really know. But this book and the Web site feel like a new beginning.

The End

So many kids with LD are too afraid to tell their story. I'm willing to tell mine. It's not the world's most exciting roller-coaster ride or anything, but it's what happened to one kid. Maybe if I open up about my problems, no matter how embarrassing they might be, other people with learning disabilities might feel free to open up about theirs. I hope the Web site can be a forum for that. But it doesn't only have to happen there.

I want to help make kids feel comfortable that it's okay to be learning disabled. They are not the only ones out there. There are other kids. There are grown-ups who are diagnosed with LD as adults. People are still finding out that they have learning disabilities, even into middle age.

Whenever I've been willing to tell my story, people usually respond. I've seen firsthand that it helps. On a sailing trip once with a group called Action Quest, I told the other kids that I was dyslexic. At the end of the trip, we all had to write letters to each other, saying what we had learned from each other. One of the other kids wrote to me and told me that he was dyslexic, too, and that I was the first person he had ever told. He felt so relieved to be able to tell me. And he never would have if I hadn't told him first.

The big thing people say is, don't be ashamed about it. The truth is that sometimes I still do feel ashamed, like when I can't go to the airport to pick up my friends even though I want to. The key isn't not to feel ashamed. The key is to realize that every-body feels ashamed sometimes, and this is just the thing that we have that sometimes makes us feel this way. It's okay to be ashamed sometimes. It's human.

And I've come to realize that I might fantasize too much about what I could be doing somewhere else. I'm starting to learn that it's hard for me to en-joy a place while I'm in it. My mom constantly tells me that I need to live in the present, to stop wonder-ing about some big future and start digging in to where I am. I think that's fair to say, even though I don't like to admit it.

Another thing people ask me is, if there were a switch I could flip to become "normal" all of a sud-den, would I flip it? I think about it every day, and the truth is that I wouldn't immediately say yes. I'd have to think about it. I have a pretty good life. And "normal" people can be assholes.

The truth is that you have to play the cards that you're dealt. We all fold sometimes. Sometimes people have the guts to ante up again. It's hard, but you have to try to be one of those people.

I struggle with it all the time. But if you ante up again, you get a new hand. Or at least a different one. As my dad would say, "Nose down, ass up, and push forward." It's our family motto.

LD kids are like slower-growing trees. We're not as fast, maybe, as some other kids are. Sometimes the strong trees sprout up really fast. But sooner or later, the other trees that haven't are going to grow, too, and eventually catch up. The trees that grow up fast might die faster than the other trees. When they're dying, other trees are just starting to grow. A lot of Bradlee men have been late bloomers. I am a late bloomer. It is okay to be a late bloomer.

The times when I am happiest are when I concentrate on the things I am good at. There are only two things I can do without screwing up: surfing and snowboarding. On the board I can never screw up, I can only learn from my mistakes. That's how you should look at life. Doing those things makes me feel normal, and alive.

Keep your mind on things like that, not on your disabilities. Don't let it get to you because you think you're a loser. Even when you see no point in living, which has happened to me many times, there are things you can do that other people can't. You just have to find them.

Every superhero has some kind of weakness. We all have our weaknesses. I guess LD kids, we like to express ourselves in a different way. Maybe God decided, "Well, if he can't learn properly, I'll give him something special that he can do. But he has to find it."

In a way, if you really think about it, everybody has a learning disability. We all have trouble learning something. When you think of learning disabled, you think of kids who have trouble reading. But learning disabled literally means that you're having trouble *learning*. And that could be learning about anything.

I have very vivid dreams, and sometimes I have nightmares about war. Fighting on Omaha Beach, for one. But the thing about all of those dreams is, out of all of them, I've survived. I think it's telling me that I'll have conflicts in my life, different hard parts, but I'll always manage to get through them. I'll make it through life, no matter how hard I have to fight.

And in those dreams, I'm never fighting alone. There are other people in the war who are fighting, too. And so it's telling me, you're not the only one who's fighting. There are other people fighting in life. I have my piece, they have theirs.

I haven't overcome being learning disabled, or having VCFS. Those aren't things you ever really overcome. You live with them. But I have come a long way.

The best thing you can be, in your heart, is good. Just good. You might feel like an ugly duckling sometimes, but that's okay. You don't have to be the best.

Just have a good heart. Because you build from that.
And it goes on.

—Quinn Bradlee,
Washington, D.C.

Acknowledgments

PublicAffairs and Me

————

My relationship with PublicAffairs isn't your regular relationship with a publisher. Peter Osnos, who founded PublicAffairs, is a very close friend of both of my parents. My dad hired Peter to work at the *Post* in 1966, and they worked together for a long time. When Peter started PublicAffairs, he asked my dad if he could use my dad's name to help him set the tone for the kind of publishing house he wanted to run, and my dad said yes. (If you look at the last page of the book, you can see what I'm talking about.) Seven years ago, Peter had the idea for me to write this book; it would never have happened without him.

But it's even more than that. Peter's son, Evan Osnos, was my camp counselor at summer camp one year, at Camp Kieve in Maine. Lindsay Jones, who is one of my oldest friends from growing up and like a sister to me, works at PublicAffairs, too, and helped us along the way. It's really kind of like a family operation, in a good way. And though I didn't know her at first, over the past year I've gotten to know Morgen van Vorst, who was our editor on this book. She was a great editor, and a very patient person. She figured out how to get the best out of me. I thank her with all of my heart. I also want to thank Whitney Peeling, who is in charge of publicity, and Susan Weinberg, the publisher, for all that they've done to help us get this book out there. Last, I want to thank Melissa Raymond, for her hard work on the production. We made a lot of changes right up until the book went to print, and she took them all with good cheer.

Plain and simple, this book wouldn't exist if it weren't for PublicAffairs. They've been really good to me throughout this whole process. To everybody who works there, to Peter and Morgen and everybody else, I just want to say: thank you.

Dr. Shprintzen:
The VCFS International Center in Syracuse, the Educational Foundation, and Success Stories

For a long time, there was very little going on in the general community that informed people about VCFS. You could say "VCFS" to people—and to some extent you still can—and people don't know what the hell you're talking about.

So, in 1994, I decided to start an educational founda- tion. I got together about twenty people, some of whom were professionals, both here and abroad, and then some fami- lies of patients. We met a few times a year, hammered out some bylaws, and eventually we incorporated in about 2000 or 2001.

Now, we have a Web site (www.vcfsef.org) that gets somewhere around 300,000 hits a year, and there are thou- sands of members worldwide. It's truly an international

*organization now, comprised of parents, patients, re-
searchers, and anyone interested in learning about VCFS.
We have large annual educational meetings, in places like
Europe and Australia. And we've reached thousands and
thousands of people, with the meetings and the Web site
combined. A number of other leading researchers in the
field—Wendy Kates, Doron Gothelf, Stephan Eliez, and
Tony Simon—are all active in the organization, and that
has really fostered collaborative information sharing and
collaborative research. We're all working on different things
together now to make advances in the field. (The Educational
Foundation doesn't fund research or patient care; that has
to be subsidized by each individual researcher, their insti-
tute, and through various granting agencies like the
National Institutes of Health.)*

*The Foundation's meetings are unique. We have par-
ents and people with VCFS and professionals, all in the same
room, listening to the same talks. We learn from the families; hopefully they learn from us. And then many of those
families serve as research subjects for projects that are going
on. In fact, some of the research studies even take place at
those meetings.*

*In general, we can use all the help that we can get. I
watch the political season with some chagrin, as the can-
didates raise millions and millions of dollars to spend tear-
ing each other down. That money could be so much better
used in so many different ways. With $2 million, the re-
search we are doing at the VCFS International Center in
Syracuse could go a long way toward curing many of the
symptoms of VCFS within five years. Moreover, the same
treatments might prove useful in treating people with sim-*

ilar ailments who don't *have VCFS. Our hope is that understanding the mechanism for mental illness and other common problems in VCFS will lead to treatments that will be applicable to millions of people worldwide who have behavioral disorders and psychiatric disease.*

I don't mean just figuring out how to treat *all the symptoms effectively. If we could figure out the molecular mechanics of what makes each symptom occur genetically, we might be able to figure out how to reverse them. The heart defects occur so early that it might be tough, but other things—the cognitive difficulties, the psychiatric difficulties—we could figure out how to reverse on the genetic level, or at least render negligibly functional. I hope, someday, as awareness of VCFS changes, that this too will change. I hope this book helps in that regard, too.*

Even where we are now, though, I just want it to be clear that there are many success stories. But first, you have to define success. There are a lot of different perspectives on life. I've learned quite a bit from my patients, and their families, in that regard.

About seven years ago, when we had our annual VCFS Educational Foundation meeting in Australia, I was asked to give a lecture. When I was done, a young lady came up to me and introduced herself. She told me that she had VCFS, which I knew as soon as she approached me. Her mother was standing behind her, not wanting to interrupt. And she asked if she could tell me a story, and I said, "Of course."

She told me that she had come to the diagnosis late, at about nineteen or so. They lived in the outback, so it was primarily a farming community, though she didn't come from a family of farmers. She struggled all through high school, but her mother really pushed hard. She really made her work. As I said before, this is really the root of most of our success stories. She graduated from high school, but she didn't have great grades. She didn't know that she had VCFS, there were no special accommodations made, and she went through the regular curriculum.

Her hopes, and her mother's hopes, for her to go to college were dashed, because she just didn't have the grades. She knew that she'd never pass the entrance exam. And so she was lost. She didn't know what she was going to do.

To kill time over the summer, she knew she had to get a job to make some money, so she got a part-time job in a veterinarian's office as a vet's assistant. And she found, within a very short period of time, that she loved it. She just really loved it. And she told me why. She said, "Look, first of all, I came in and I didn't really need to deal with people very much during the course of the day. I was working with animals." And because this was the outback, it wasn't just small animals. It was sheep, horses, cows; there were stalls to clean out, a significant amount of hard physical labor involved, and she had to feed and clean them and walk them and exercise them, too.

And she said, "I learned quickly that when I was kind to the animals, they were kind to me. They loved to see me coming. And I just, I woke up in the morning looking forward to my day. And I worked hard at it."

The vet saw how good she was at what she was doing, and how much she enjoyed it. This was unusual, because a vet's assistant is often a temporary job for people, college students or high school kids, who might be there for a year or so. It's not a career path for most people. But the vet saw how much she loved it, and he offered her a full-time job, and she took it.

She told me, "You know, I'm not making a lot of money, but I'm making enough money to have my own apartment." She lived not far from her mother, and went over to her mother's house for dinner a couple of times a week. She had a car: She drove to her mother's, she drove to work. She didn't take driving trips, because she knew that she wouldn't be able to handle that. But if she knew where she was going, she'd be fine. She had carved out her niche. She had made a life for herself, and she was telling me this in great detail. And her mother is standing about ten feet behind her, she's crying already. And then this young woman said, "And I just want you to know that the reason I'm telling you this, is I just want to let you know: I'm happy."

It was like somebody hit me between the eyes with a two-by-four. That she summed it all up by just saying that she was happy. I have two grown kids, two very different kids, but what do I want for them? To be happy. In this particular instance, this young lady found her place. She took a job that most people wouldn't regard as a "career," but she loved it, and she was happy. How many people can say confidently that they are happy?

What it comes down to is: Do you love your child to pieces? Do you want the best for your child? Do you come up making a decision where they do in fact find their niche? I've seen it happen with many of my patients with VCFS, and I've also seen it not happen, where parents have unrealistic expectations of what they want for their kids. We've learned enough about the syndrome to say, "I don't think I'd go there," versus, "That sounds like a really good thing." We've seen more than a few good things for our patients. People with VCFS are not so far outside of the norm that they don't fit in anywhere. The challenge is finding that place.

A Little More about
FriendsOfQuinn.com
from the folks at
HealthCentral.com

Quinn Bradlee first dreamed up the idea of a website for people living with learning disabilities while he was writing *A Different Life.* As he shared his own story, Quinn came to understand how valuable it was to communicate his experience with others, and started to think about the incredible potential for a community where learning disabled individuals could share their experiences. He thought about how isolated and alone he had felt at times, and how having one person to talk to—one

Front page of FriendsOfQuinn.com

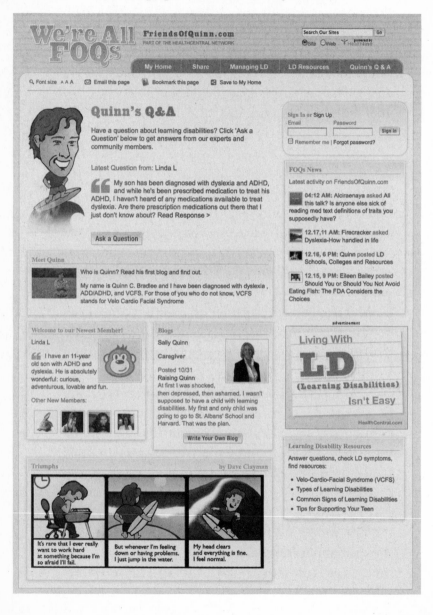

who listened and understood what he was going through—made all the difference in the world. Quinn recognized the need for a safe and supportive place for everyone who felt just a little different, where they could come together to learn, share stories, and exchange support and advice. It was with this goal in mind that Quinn joined the team at Health Central.com, and launched FriendsOfQuinn.com.

Living with LD isn't always easy, but sometimes the difficulties can make a person's achievements all the more meaningful. As Quinn describes in his book, he finds himself at his absolute best when he's out on his surfboard catching a wave, or carving down the mountain on a snowboard. Quinn will share his triumphs regularly, and will encourage members to contribute their own success stories.

You can connect with the FriendsOfQuinn.com community by creating and customizing your own profile and by keeping a blog, which can be updated as often as you like. Your blog can be used for expressing your thoughts, sharing bits of wisdom, or getting creative—uploading photos, drawings, or videos. You can also connect with others by visiting Quinn's Q&A, where you can ask questions of medical experts and people who are well-versed in the trials and tribulations of managing a learning disability.

The more individuals understand their learning disabilities, the easier it is for them to navigate their lives from day to day. And the more others understand what LD individuals are going through, the easier it is to offer support and encouragement. FriendsOfQuinn.com will provide the best resources to help manage learning disabilities, including clinical information (treatment options, medication side effects) and lifestyle tips (locating the best schools, getting a job, dating) from a range of experts and peers.

FriendsOfQuinn.com is part of The Health-Central Network. Like all of HealthCentral's 35+ sites, FriendsOfQuinn.com is focused on the people who manage their condition day-to-day.

F.A.Q. on FOQ

What is FriendsOfQuinn.com?

FriendsOfQuinn.com is a networking and educational resource for anyone living with or caring for an individual with learning disabilities. The site is focused on young adults who are dealing with issues associated with learning disabilities, including but not limited to stigma, dating, bullying, medication side effects, frustration with school, and family issues.

How do I get involved with the site?
Can I participate?

Anyone over thirteen years of age can get involved with FriendsOfQuinn.com. And you can participate in a number of different ways: share your story or advice in your own blog on the site, ask questions of experts and community members, or browse our library of medical information, educational resources, and tips for daily living.

Why would I get involved?

If you live with learning disabilities or care for someone with LD, have an interest in meeting others who understand what you're going through, or are looking for information or advice about diagnosis, treatment, medication, accommodations, condition management, or other aspects of living with LD, FriendsOfQuinn.com offers up a wealth of resources. And it's free.

What are experts?

When it comes to your health, often experience and empathy are as important as medical advice. That's why we not only hire the top health professionals in their field, but we are also committed to involving expert patients and expert caregivers who are passionate about raising awareness and supporting others with LD.

How can I keep my identity safe?

When you register with FriendsOfQuinn.com, you will be asked to create a username and enter your email address. Please note that your username can be any name you choose (provided it's not already taken), and your email address will never be shared with anyone else on, or off, the site unless you choose to do so. All those who register to use FriendsOfQuinn.com must be at least thirteen years old.

I have special reading needs; will I still be able to use the site?

FriendsOfQuinn.com has been designed with a slightly larger font and less clutter than most sites to make it easier to read and navigate. You can also increase the font size on every page with the click of a button.

For more information on FriendsOfQuinn.com, please contact qbradlee@thcn.com.

Quinn Bradlee was born in 1982 with velo-cardio-facial syndrome (VCFS), the second-most-prevalent genetic syndrome in the world behind Down syndrome. As a result, he has battled severe physical ailments and learning disabilities throughout his life. Quinn attended the Lab School, in Washington, D.C., for twelve years, and then graduated from the Gow School in South Wales, New York. He has also attended the Landmark School Summer Program, Landmark College, American University, and the New York Film Academy. He has since worked as a documentaty filmmaker, with a focus on short documentary films about children with learning disabilities and rare genetic syndromes. In the fall of 2008, he launched a Web site, www.FriendsOfQuinn.com, to create an online community for LD kids and their families. He is the son of Ben Bradlee, the former executive editor of *The Washington Post,* and Sally Quinn, journalist and best-selling author, who is the co-moderator of the On Faith segment of www.washingtonpost.com. He lives next door to his parents in Washington, D.C.

Jeff Himmelman has worked on two national bestsellers, Bob Woodward's *Maestro* and Tim Russert's *Big Russ and Me,* in addition to a host of other book projects as an editor, ghostwriter, and author. His work with Mr. Woodward and a team of other reporters helped *The Washington Post* secure the national affairs Pulitzer Prize for its post–9/11 coverage, and he received a front-page byline in the *Post* for his work on the "Ten Days in September" series documenting the Bush administration's initial response to the attacks. At present, he is writing a book about Quinn's father, the legendary *Post* editor Ben Bradlee, for Random House. He is also a professional musician who writes, records, and performs under the band name Down Dexter. He lives in Washington, D.C., with his wife, Kirsten Lodal, who is the CEO of National Student Partnerships, a national anti-poverty organization.